The Career
Playbook

The Career Playbook

Essential Advice
for Today's Aspiring
Young Professional

JAMES M. CITRIN

CROWN
BUSINESS

New York

Copyright © 2015 by Esaress International S. A. R. L.

All rights reserved.

Published in the United States by Crown Business, an imprint of the Crown Publishing Group, a division of Penguin Random House LLC, New York. www.crownpublishing.com

CROWN BUSINESS is a trademark and CROWN and the Rising Sun colophon are registered trademarks of Penguin Random House LLC.

Crown Business books are available at special discounts for bulk purchases for sales promotions or corporate use. Special editions, including personalized covers, excerpts of existing books, or books with corporate logos, can be created in large quantities for special needs. For more information, contact Premium Sales at (212) 572-2232 or e-mail specialmarkets@randomhouse.com.

Library of Congress Cataloging-in-Publication Data is available upon request.

ISBN 978-0-553-44696-8
eBook ISBN 978-0-553-44697-5

Printed in the United States of America

Charts and graphs illustrated by Fred Haynes
Illustrations by Annalora von Pentz
Cover design by FORT

10 9 8 7 6 5 4 3 2 1

First Edition

To my beloved kids

Teddy, Oliver, and Lily

CONTENTS

The Career
Playbook

INTRODUCTION

Essential Advice for Today's Aspiring Young Professional

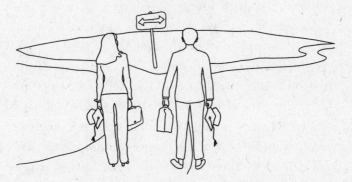

My twenty-seven-year-old niece, Alex, is remarkable. For her master's thesis at the Maryland Institute College of Art, she conceived of and brought to life *Until Now*, a magazine about coming of age. Inside the attractive matte pages, forty-two writers and artists, mostly in their twenties, express their reflections, anxieties, and dreams about moving into adulthood and making their way in the world. The topics range from love and relationships, to weight control and body image, and, of course, to finding a job, forging a career, and pursuing success. I have a deep appreciation for just how hard it is for people starting out in their careers to figure out life, to land a good job, and to pursue their dreams and become the person they want to be. Even the best educated, most ambitious, most creative, and most energetic find it difficult to know where to turn to get the right advice.

Nathaniel, twenty-eight, graduated from Harvard in 2008 with honors in history and literature. Rather than following the well-worn path that runs from the Ivy League to a career in investment banking or consulting, he opted to join the analytics team at an online media start-up with only ten employees. After working in start-ups for four years, Nathaniel decided to attend the MIT Sloan School of Management, where he took a graduate internship at Google and was offered a full-time job at the program's end. But Nathaniel was conflicted about the offer. If he had his way, he would join yet another start-up in market analytics. He knew that Google would give him the chance to work with smart people, but he wanted the breadth and hands-on experience offered by early-stage companies. At the same time, could he really pass up the prestige, stability, and future opportunities that would inevitably await him at Google? And what if the start-up he joined didn't make it? Would he find himself out of work and ruing the day he'd turned down Google's offer?

Nathaniel didn't know how to decide. Should he follow the classic career wisdom of starting at a blue-chip company, taking advantage of its resources and of the benefits that come from being associated with a top organization? Or should he go with his instincts and make his way back into the adrenaline-filled environment of a start-up?

His decision wasn't an easy one, and you too will experience decisions like this at more than one point in your career. No one—absolutely no one—can predict how your career will unfold. But I can say this with confidence. As your career unfolds, it will make many unexpected twists and turns. It will be a winding road, not a straight line.

When successful people give advice or tell the story of their careers, they often speak in a way that makes it seem as if their success was inevitable. But when you're dealing with the reality of trying to secure an interview, deciding which job to pursue or accept, worrying about money, and looking for that entry-level position that will open the door to future opportunities in your chosen field, nothing is clear. Certainty exists only in hindsight, when you're looking back on the decisions and actions you took that eventually led to career success.

One person who exemplifies this fact is Jim Meyer, CEO of Sirius XM. When Jim was growing up, his family moved around frequently because his father was a career officer in the U.S. Navy. Because of this, Jim had no choice but to learn how to adapt to different cultures and constantly make new friends. Jim went on to attend St. Bonaventure University in New York, majoring in economics and later receiving his MBA there as well before taking a job at RCA Corporation, a leading manufacturer of television sets at the time. Through RCA's history of changing ownership (the company was sold to General Electric and later to Thomson Consumer Electronics Company), Jim was fortunate to be involved with the company, Thomson, that was a partner in the early days of the creation of DIRECTV. His career bloomed over the course of twenty years, in which he oversaw the production of high-end color televisions and became the company's COO.

Jim did well financially and was ready to retire after he left the company in 2001. But a couple of years later, a friend and former boss who was also integrally involved in the launch of DIRECTV became CEO of Sirius Satellite Radio and asked Jim to come on board as a consultant. Jim accepted, and in 2004 he went further, joining the company on a full-time basis to run its operations and sales efforts. Jim's focus was working with car manufacturers in Detroit, Germany, and Japan to make Sirius players a regular feature for new models; this would become the company's core strategy for early growth. Jim is a low-key, authentic person who always demonstrates care for those around him, and people throughout the company were highly motivated to work for him. After Sirius merged with XM Satellite Radio in 2008, the company's board promoted him to CEO in 2012.

You wouldn't know it by looking at his job title today, but Jim's career, like most people's, was a winding and unexpected road. His story also shows that you don't need to attend Stanford or Oxford, or work at Google or Goldman Sachs, in order to accomplish something significant. As long as you make sound decisions, work incredibly hard, support others, build meaningful relationships, and have some good luck, you'll have a good shot at achievement and success.

In *The Career Playbook*, I am sharing everything I've learned about successful careers from working intimately with some of the most successful chief executives, entrepreneurs, not-for-profit leaders, and gurus around the world. My goal is to present this essential advice in a way that will be relevant to anyone motivated to pursue success in today's hypercompetitive, fast-changing, and confusing world.

The Job Market Today

The career marketplace for new graduates and millennials (the approximately 82 million people born between 1981 and about 2000) has never been more competitive, unstructured, and difficult to navigate. For every appealing entry-level professional position in a given industry, there are dozens, often hundreds, and sometimes thousands of candidates.

> "I've been subject to strange and otherwise off-putting treatment from potential employers that I can only categorize as jaded and bitter. They seem to make it their goal to discourage people my age from reaching as high as they can."[1]
>
> **—ALEX, TWENTY-SEVEN**

If you are a new entrant into the job market, you are consumed by such questions as how to break through the crowd of applicants to land an interview, how to figure out which jobs to pursue, and how to obtain the right introductions, become noticed, and get your shot

---

[1] Throughout the book, these quotes are from aspiring young professionals sharing their thoughts, frustrations, and questions about managing their careers.

at a job in the first place. Every year Google receives over 3 *million* applicants through its website. In 2013, 57,000 people applied to Teach for America, undeterred by its grueling application process and 10 percent acceptance rate. At the most prestigious financial institutions and consulting firms, the numbers are even more competitive. For each of the 17,000 college students who apply to Goldman Sachs, for example, just 350 make the cut. Morgan Stanley received about 90,000 applications for its 1,000 summer spots for analysts and associates in 2014, and 80 percent who received offers accepted on the spot. McKinsey has a 200 to 1 application-to-offer ratio, and roughly 90 percent accept offers to work at the firm. With a 0.5 percent to 2 percent acceptance rate into these programs, it is easier to be admitted to Harvard (with its 5.9 percent admit rate). And even outside the technology, finance, and consulting fields, competition is just as ferocious. Johnson & Johnson, consistently rated as one of the world's most admired companies (ranked #12 on LinkedIn's Global Most In-Demand Employers), receives over 180,000 applications each year for the approximately 720 positions the company hires directly from colleges and universities (a 0.4 percent acceptance rate).[2] Over the past two years, the insurance giant MetLife has received an average of 151,000 applications for the 2,464 entry-level positions it has filled (a 1.6 percent acceptance rate). The same

---

[2] J&J fills approximately 6 percent of its external hiring directly from universities (the 720 positions a year); for each position it receives between 200 and 300 applications. J&J will hire approximately 18,000 employees in 2014, of whom approximately 12,000 will be recruited from outside the company.

pattern holds true for leading not-for-profit organizations. For its most recent fiscal year, the American Red Cross filled 2,900 entry-level positions from 67,500 applicants (a 4 percent acceptance rate).[3]

We've all heard stories of recent graduates being forced to move back in with their parents after applying unsuccessfully for scores of jobs, or settling for minimum-wage jobs or positions they are overqualified for that they wouldn't have even considered before college. Of the more than 3 million college graduates who entered the U.S. workforce in 2013, nearly half accepted jobs for which they believed they were overqualified. In 2012, according to the Federal Reserve Bank of New York, 44 percent of recent graduates were working in positions that typically don't require a college degree, up from 34 percent in 2001. Why? Because recent graduates are desperate to find a job—*any job*—to pay the bills. Finding a position that will lead to a promising career path is considered a luxury that many simply cannot afford. Those fortunate enough to land a job in the postrecession market of 2010 and 2011 were forced to take almost a 20 percent pay cut from prerecession levels. And when you start in a financial hole like this, your earnings can lag for years, even after the job market recovers. Companies tend to make their compensation awards on the basis of where you were previously

---

[3] To be more precise, of the 2,900 entry-level positions at the American Red Cross. 1,800 are phlebotomists, blood donation technicians, who draw blood all day long. There are approximately 27,000 applicants for those positions, a 7 percent acceptance rate; for all other positions, the competition is even greater, with a 2.7 percent acceptance rate.

and what salary you made there. All of these pressures are further exacerbated by the challenge of student loans, with the average college graduate now carrying a debt of nearly $30,000. The combination of underemployment and significant college debt can be toxic. It helps to explain why young people are delaying home ownership (just 36 percent of households under age thirty-five own a home, down from 41 percent in 2008, according to the U.S. Census).

At the same time, the sale of WhatsApp to Facebook for $19 billion (that was $350 million per each of the company's fifty-five employees) makes recent graduates and people in the early stages of their careers rethink whether they should even try to follow a traditional career path. Today is the golden age of the start-up (for the time being), where it seems as if any talented, ambitious person with initiative and an idea can strike it rich—or at least get a job—by founding a start-up and selling it to a large company. If you're an entrepreneurial person, why not try to found a company that gets "acquihired" by a large company like Google, Yahoo!, Facebook, or Twitter (each of which acquired between twenty-five and sixty companies from 2012 to 2014)? Many small companies—for example, mobile app developers like Stamped, OnTheAir, GoPollGo, Alike, Spindle, Lucky Sort, and Posterous—were acquired for their talent and had their services shut down and their teams integrated into the acquiring companies.

The structure of career paths has changed, as have the tools of job searching. You want a well-paid job, of course, but most people starting out in the work world today also want to be associated with an organization that aligns with their values and makes them proud. You want a job that offers you the opportunity to achieve the lifestyle you want to live—to be able ultimately to afford the things a well-paid job leads to, like a comfortable house, a nice car, travel, and entertainment.

You want to be respected. You want a chance to show what you can do, be challenged, and grow in your job or organization. And more than any previous generation, you want to work on something meaningful, to make a difference. Along with this, you want the flexibility and freedom to live where you want to live and pursue your interests outside work. You realize that you are likely to work for many different employers over your career. But you welcome the opportunity to join an established company that offers security and training programs that will grow your skills and set you on the right path in your career.

Core Principles

The good news is that, although the job market today is less structured than ever before, there still are core principles that can help you achieve success in your career. If you understand and apply these principles, they will help position you to land the right job and thrive over the long term. Some principles are timeless, such as the importance of relationships in finding a job, getting ahead, and living a happy and fulfilled life. Some are less obvious, such as focusing on the success of others as much as your own career success. In the pages ahead, I'll talk about how to get around the dreaded Permission Paradox, where you can't get the job without the experience but you can't get the experience without the job. I'll offer market-tested interview strategies that will allow you to tell your story and to answer and ask questions in a way that will help you get the job. I'll discuss how to cultivate a mentor, someone who can be an invaluable source of advice, encouragement, feedback, and introductions.

In *The Career Playbook*, I'll discuss all of these principles for success and show how they affect your career in today's job marketplace.

- In Part 1, I'll discuss *how careers really work*, offering a road map for how to think about your career and the roles of money, meaning, networks, and relationships.
- In Part 2, I'll show readers *how to get the job:* how to secure and perform well in interviews, how to overcome the catch-22 of the Permission Paradox; how, if you have or are getting a degree in the liberal arts, to compete with those with technical and preprofessional degrees (business, finance, etc.); and how to decide what job to accept.
- In Part 3, I convey, on the basis of my experience of placing some of the most prominent and successful leaders, *how to thrive* in your career—how to get off to the right start in a new job, how to be an inspiring leader, how to progress swiftly and surely on your career

path, and how to cultivate a mentor, among other things.

A Unique Vantage Point on Careers

Through my twenty-one years of executive search and leadership advisory work at Spencer Stuart, I've had a privileged perspective on how careers are built and success is achieved. I've led the recruitments of over 600 executives of giant corporations, early-stage companies, educational institutions, and not-for-profits, ranging from the CEOs of Intel, PayPal, Hulu, and the New York Times Company to the MIT Media Lab, the New York Public Library, and Product (RED).

I also have conducted thousands and thousands of interviews over the last thirty-five years. I started as an admissions office interviewer as a senior at Vassar College, then helped lead recruiting as an analyst and associate on Wall Street and later in management consulting. At Spencer Stuart I've done an estimated five thousand executive interviews in my twenty years at the company. I've sat in boardrooms hundreds of times facilitating and observing clients interview CEO and board candidates and other senior executives. So trust me when I say that I've seen both the great *and* the less than great when it comes to interviewing.

Along with my recruitment work, I've had the opportunity to give career advice to people working across the full gamut of industries and circumstances—from top executives to college students, MBAs, and unemployed middle managers; from successful CEOs, government leaders, and military leaders to befuddled teenagers and individuals trying to recover from reputational disgrace. Through this experience, I've been able to learn what advice really works and what words are vapid or ineffective.

Research Base

Building on my professional experience, in writing this book I've explored rigorous new research in order to find customized insights for young professionals. My research team and I conducted hundreds of interviews with senior business and not-for-profit leaders, corporate chief human resources officers, and career development directors from top colleges and universities. None of the contributions were more important, however, than what I learned from brainstorming with, advising, and listening to the scores of young professionals and college and graduate students whom I've had the opportunity to work with. These include my three kids, ages twenty-five, twenty-three, and twenty, and dozens of their friends, classmates, and associates.

In addition, we conducted two related surveys that illuminated many of the insights in this book. The first survey was targeted to young professionals, with whom we explored key factors about careers, including future expectations, attitudes about job satisfaction and personal fulfillment, actions in the workplace that influenced success, trade-offs between different attributes of a job, and how to cultivate a mentor.[4] Second, we created a "sibling" survey for top business and not-for-profit leaders in which we asked parallel questions designed to find areas of alignment or misalignment on matters that explain career success.[5]

My Goal for This Book

The Career Playbook is dedicated to you, the aspiring young professional who is launching a career and looking to carve out a distinctive place in the world over your first decade after graduation. My goal is that this book will speak to your personal situation and provide

---

[4] We distributed the young professional survey over the course of 2014 online via LinkedIn and Facebook and by e-mail to a panel of young professionals and their friends. We also partnered with Indiana University, Vassar College, Wesleyan University, Dartmouth College, and several other leading colleges and universities to survey their young alumni. From this outreach, we received over two thousand completed surveys from respondents in thirty-three states in the United States and multiple countries. The overwhelming majority of respondents were between the ages of eighteen and thirty-two; 60 percent were female and 40 percent were male. With this number of completed surveys, the data are extremely powerful and robust.

[5] The top leader survey was completed by far fewer, approximately one hundred, with each leader personally invited by me. They include some household name CEOs and entrepreneurs as well as others you may not have heard of. In speaking with market research experts, I was advised to point out that while this is a small sample from which to draw statistical conclusions, I believe it is a representative broad cross section of the most distinguished and successful professionals today.

you with the most effective, actionable, and market-tested strategies for maximizing your professional success and personal satisfaction.

> "I have recently realized I need to get more focused on my career. I've turned a corner where my inability to support myself was frustrating and I longed for financial independence. And financial independence comes from a good career."
>
> —HALEY, TWENTY-FOUR

Even when career opportunities are plentiful and you have multiple alternatives, sorting out how to think about your choices, what to do and what actions to take, is still a high-stakes game fraught with confusion and potential career land mines. It's an unfortunate fact that career decisions tend to be made on the basis of uncertain and incomplete information and often under significant time, financial, and emotional pressure. Too often, the lessons that would have served you well during the decision become clear only in hindsight.

If you are going through a job transition, you know it's really hard. But it can be done. Truly. Down the road, after you have acted on the advice in this book and told your story, I hope that your success and happiness will seem to have been inevitable all along.

Part 1

HOW CAREERS REALLY *WORK*

1

THE SIX PHASES OF YOUR CAREER

As you enter the workforce and in the early days of your career, chances are that you will have some notion about how you expect your work life to unfold. You might have ambitious, fairly concrete goals—to become a senior executive in a corporation, a partner in a professional firm, or a leader of a nonprofit that provides housing for people in need. Or you might be saving your aspirations for later, focusing now on just finding a job. Whichever the case, from the vantage point of this formative time in your career, it's often difficult to connect the dots between where you are today and where you hope to be in the future. And yet it's natural to ask yourself questions like "How am I doing?" and "Am I at the right place at this point in my career?" or "Am I learning and achieving what I need to move to the next level?"

In the introduction, I talked about how your career is more likely to follow a winding road than a straight line. While everyone's individual career path is different, and the specifics of yours will be as unique as your fingerprint, most people go through a common series of six phases over the course of their career. Understanding these phases, as well as how you are valued, what is expected of you, and what you need to deliver in each phase, will offer a useful road map to help you see where you are in your career and how you are performing. Here are the six phases of a career that I've seen, across the countless number of people I've worked with.

The Six Career Phases

1. Aspiration Phase
2. Promise Phase
3. Momentum Phase
4. Harvest Phase
5. Encore Phase
6. Legacy Phase

How Employers Value You: Potential and Experience

Your value to your employer changes following a pattern strikingly similar to how physicists describe the properties of energy. They refer to potential energy (energy at rest) and kinetic energy (energy in motion). Careers follow similar patterns. As you prepare to enter the workforce, you are building up your store of potential value—the value you will be able to add in the future by exercising your intellectual and interpersonal energies, applying your education and academic achievements, and bringing your enthusiasm, work ethic, and energy to an organization. As you land your first few jobs and begin to gain experience, this potential is translated into momentum, as you become increasingly more valuable on the basis of your professional expertise, reputation, and track record. Picture a kid on a swing, kicking his legs so that he swings higher and higher. That is how your career takes off.

You launch your career with the scale registering heavy on potential and light on experience. As you move through your career, the scale shifts and the experience side eventually grows to outweigh the potential side. The trick is to add to the experience side of the equation without emptying the potential side. The more you can turn your potential value into valuable experiences, which can then be converted into greater potential, the more valuable you will become in the career market over time.

Now let's turn to the six phases that most careers follow. For the purpose of this book, we are primarily interested in the first three phases, as you seek out and launch your career, so we'll spend most of our time on those.

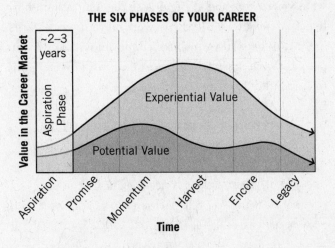

THE SIX PHASES OF YOUR CAREER

Aspiration

This phase, beginning in your college years and continuing through your first years in the workforce, marks your transition into adulthood. It draws on everything you've learned in college and internships and all of the challenges you will meet or will have faced in your first exposures to the work world. The Aspiration Phase is about discovery and introspection, the process of learning, and the development of knowledge. It is the time when you are getting your earliest experiences that will inform your interests and strengths. In this phase, your value in the career market is based almost completely on your potential. So the most important objective is to discover your strengths and interests and to begin learning marketable skills. Try out as many different kinds of tasks and jobs as possible. Get feedback from professors, peers, and mentors who can help you to identify what you are good at—and what you're *not* good at. If you use the Aspiration Phase to gain exposure, build skills, work on your weaknesses, and fill in gaps in your knowledge, you will build your potential and strengthen your ability to provide value to current and future employers.

> "I am getting to the point where my future isn't just theoretical. It's happening. It's now. And I have to figure out ways to get what I want. I think a huge part of early career success is admitting that it's in your hands. Not in your college counselor's hands or your mentor's hands. It's up to you."
>
> —DOUG, TWENTY-THREE

In the Aspiration Phase, you won't have much of the industry-specific knowledge that you'll gain as your career unfolds. So focus on acquiring life skills that are valued in every industry: writing, thinking critically, listening well, solving problems, and collaborating effectively with others. And don't forget to focus attention on your life outside work. Take the time to build meaningful friendships, establish healthy living habits, and partake in activities you enjoy. These skills, coupled with the ones you'll develop at work, are the foundation of any successful career and life. If you build them now, you'll be poised for success as you develop more specialized skills later on, starting in the Promise Phase.

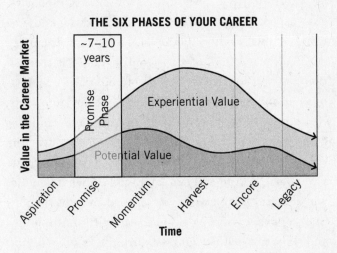

THE SIX PHASES OF YOUR CAREER

Promise

The Promise Phase begins with your first or second job and lasts through your early promotions and job changes. Chronologically, this phase tends to run from one or two years after graduation over the next seven to ten years of your career. During this stage, your value will begin to be recognized by those who employ you through your compensation, promotions, and access to the best assignments and mentors. You will continue to explore your interests and talents, but you will also begin to develop specific professional skills and make meaningful contributions to your organization.

One goal in this phase is to show that the bet your superiors made on your potential was well placed. You will do that by becoming known as a can-do person who meets deadlines, does high-quality work no matter the assignment, and asks good questions. Employers want employees who are enthusiastic, responsive, curious, helpful, optimistic, and hardworking and who work well with others, both above and below them.

The second goal of the Promise Phase is to position yourself for the next stage of your career by testing out a diverse set of roles and work environments. Remember that you can expect to work for as many as fifteen to twenty organizations or businesses over the course of your career. As long as you have a rationale for experimenting and can later explain what you did, why you did it, and what you learned from it, then it's fine to have a winding career path, with multiple left and right turns. Push yourself during this stage to find out the answers to questions such as whether you prefer working on your own, in small project teams, or in larger organizations and whether, in all honesty, you are willing to put up with the late-night and weekend work required for jobs in lucrative sectors like technology and financial services. Reflect on whether you thrive in competitive environments, where there are stars and also-rans, or prefer cultures that put a premium on teamwork, or seniority. Consider whether you are comfortable with ambiguity and having your results depend on things outside your control or whether you prefer the structure of well-defined roles or the fulfillment of task completion.

There are two other critical questions you want to address during the Promise Phase, the answers to which will lead you toward different career paths. First, are you inclined toward a position whose objective is to generate revenue, or do you prefer support functions? Second, are you skilled and interested in managing others, or do you prefer to be more of an individual contributor? Often answers to these questions emerge only over time. You may need to switch departments, companies, and even industries to answer them, and you should reflect upon them carefully over the first decade of your career. If you've built a strong foundation of work relationships and a reputation for excellent work, you may well be able to switch jobs within your existing organization to explore these key questions.

You chose your academic major during the Aspiration Phase. The Promise Phase is when you declare your professional major (which may or may not have anything to do with the academic major from college) and figure out the roles and settings that will allow you to be most successful and most true to yourself. This stage isn't limited to a particular age range. Given how careers are structured today, with serial entrepreneurism and the lure of start-ups, and with corporate training programs the rare exception and lifetime employment a relic of a bygone era, it is highly likely that you will be switching roles and companies more frequently than in the past in order to test out the different settings and roles. If you can expect to work in fifteen to twenty companies or organizations, you will need to count on having multiple starts or restarts. It is incumbent on you to figure out the best environments and roles in the Promise Phase so you can dig into your chosen area and start becoming valued for your track record and experience. This is to say that there is one other key goal of the Promise Phase—to develop your skills in managing your own career.

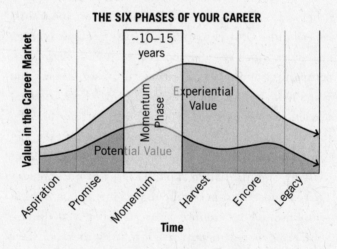

THE SIX PHASES OF YOUR CAREER

Momentum

This phase tends to run from your early thirties through your early or midforties, when you establish your track record and reputation in the marketplace. This can be in functions like marketing, finance, sales, operations, information technology, or strategy. The Momentum Phase is when the value of your experience will overtake your potential value as you increase your professional standing by capitalizing on your experience, stature, skills, and expertise. In doing this, you will become promotable in your company and more recruitable in your industry and across sectors.

Sandi Peterson, group worldwide chairman of Johnson & Johnson, is a textbook example of someone who used the Momentum Phase to position herself for even greater success (she was named #20 on the Fortune Most Powerful Women list in 2014). A government major at Cornell, Sandi focused on international economics and politics over the course of her Aspiration and Promise phases. After graduating from college, she worked in a handful of international political risk consulting firms in New York and went on to earn a master's degree from Princeton in applied economics. Following graduate school, she decided to take her interest in economics, politics, and science policy and redirect it onto a business track. She became one of the first non-MBA associates at McKinsey, where over six years as a management consultant she developed a specialization in consumer and technology companies, focusing on strategic marketing and innovation. After McKinsey, Sandi leveraged these areas of experience into new opportunities, joining Whirlpool's strategy and product development team, and three years later moving to become Nabisco's executive vice president for research and development.

Sandi's track record and reputation brought her to the attention of other companies, and she was soon recruited from the consumer products industry to the health care field, where she could apply her experience in a new sector. She joined Merck-Medco as the top marketing executive and after six years was recruited to the German life sciences company Bayer AG to lead its global health care divisions in New York. In 2012, eight years later, Sandi was recruited to Johnson & Johnson, the world's largest health care company, where today she is its number two executive. In total, Sandi oversees more than $20 billion in revenue and approximately seventy thousand people, more than half of J&J's total workforce.

Beyond leveraging your experience into new opportunities, success in the Momentum Phase is also defined by the quality of the teams you build and manage. This is perhaps the first thing CEOs and HR officers consider when deciding whether you're a fit for an executive role at the company. You want to become known as a "talent magnet," someone who has built a positive culture inside your organization, attracted world-class talent from the outside, developed talent internally, and used all of these resources to create highly effective teams. As J. Patrick Doyle, CEO of Domino's Pizza, explains, "In your mid- to late thirties, the basis of how you are judged fundamentally changes. You're no longer evaluated as an individual contributor, but rather on the quality of the people that you can attract to work with and for you."

Build goodwill by supporting those around you and being a positive, responsive, and helpful colleague and leader. This is especially important when life inevitably gets in the way during this period of your career. The more goodwill that you have built up from having supported others around you and from having been a positive, responsive, and helpful colleague and leader, the more assistance you will in turn benefit from when it comes to maintaining your momentum and balancing work with the major events in your personal life, such as marriage, parenthood, and health issues, to name a few.

The Latter Three Phases: Harvest, Encore, and Legacy

If *The Career Playbook* can help you optimize the Aspiration, Promise, and Momentum phases of your career, then we will all be able to declare it a major success. Even though the latter parts of your career seem an eternity away, let me briefly define the final three phases that most careers follow:

- **The Harvest Phase.** This phase kicks in at about your twentieth college reunion and runs for the next ten to twenty years, depending on which industry sector you're working in and how you are progressing.
- **The Encore Phase.** This stage follows traditional corporate retirement. It is well known that careers are no longer ending like clockwork at the age of sixty-five.
- **The Legacy Phase.** Finally, there is the Legacy Phase. You might think about this as the new age of retirement to leisure given lengthening life spans and longer terms of employment.

If you are interested in the details of these phases, turn to Appendix A. For now, the key points are that in these latter phases careers begin to diverge most dramatically: some people keep growing personally and professionally, moving into new positions, and redefining roles, while others start to fade. The key principle in the latter parts of your career is to find ways to redefine your experiences and apply them in new and hopefully valuable contexts.

—⊖—

The shape of your career trajectory can be quite different depending on what direction you take, how you perform, and what decisions you make along the way. For example, if you follow a traditional career in business where you focus on one field and become fairly specialized, the slope of your value in the career market can be quite steep, on both the upside and—if you don't find a way to reconceive your experience—the downside. No matter what shape your career takes, by understanding the six career phases and knowing what to focus on in each phase you will be saved a lot of soul searching when you're in the throes of trying to meet your daily demands, find new opportunities, and build a meaningful life outside the office.

A final thought as you consider the six phases from today's career vantage point. The further away you move from the Aspiration and Promise phases of your career, the more you can also expect nostalgia to kick in. You will inevitably yearn for all the uncertainty, the drama, and the sheer sense of possibility that you felt when you were an aspiring young professional.

THE CAREER TRIANGLE: JOB, COMPENSATION, AND LIFESTYLE

The Bermuda Triangle is a roughly 1-million-square-mile expanse between the picturesque Atlantic island for which it's named, Miami, Florida, and San Juan, Puerto Rico. It has reportedly enveloped wayward ships and airplanes for centuries. Happily, the Career Triangle is much more benign. But it can be challenging to navigate just the same.

In the previous chapter, I discussed the ways in which employers value you at various points in your career. Now it's time to turn to the ways in which *you* value your employers. There are three broad factors to consider when trying to determine which job or career is right for you. These three factors constitute the Career Triangle: job satisfaction, compensation, and the lifestyle that your job allows you to lead.

1. **Job Satisfaction.** This involves the nature of the position, how much will you learn and develop, and how fundamentally interested you are in the sector and business. It also has to do with how prestigious the organization is and how proud you are to be associated with the products, services, or brand.

2. **Compensation.** This includes your salary and potential for bonuses, as well as benefits like health insurance and 401k plans. It also includes any equity, options, or long-term incentive compensation.

3. **Lifestyle.** This has to do with how the job fits into your life—or how your life fits into the job. How long are the working hours? Is the organization located in a city where you would enjoy living? What is the commute like? How much control do you have over your schedule? How much travel is involved? How intense are the deadlines and crunch times?

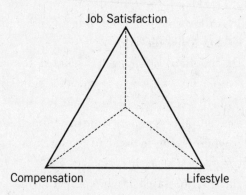

You *Can* Have It All Eventually . . . Just Not Necessarily Now

The good news is that you can achieve high marks in all three areas; the bad news is that you can't necessarily have them all now, in the early stages of your career. Job satisfaction, money, and lifestyle are almost always at odds with one another, and this is especially true as you start your career. Sometimes you'll need to work long hours for a job that pays well. And you may reach a point where you feel you've had to "sell out" on your dreams in order to make a lot of money. Or perhaps you found a job that pays decently and gives you control over your schedule, but the job itself is drudgery, or at least is unexciting.

Trade-offs are often a necessary evil. But the more you consciously think about each of the three factors and decide what is most important to you, the better you will weather each career phase and make the right decisions about your future.

The Career Triangle Through the Different Phases

Your Career Triangle changes shape over time, depending on where you are in your professional development. Let's take a look at how the triangle might look in the Aspiration Phase.

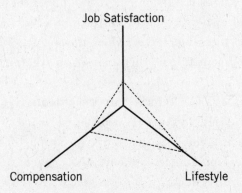

Job Satisfaction

Compensation   Lifestyle

In the early years of your career, you're focused on exploration, self-discovery, and the process of learning new skills. Because of this, there is no point in hoping to maximize your income or impact on the company. Of course you want to be challenged in your job, but you know that many of the tasks you'll work on in this phase are things that simply need to get done. Your work will be far less strategic than what the most senior people are working on, and it may well be less intellectually stimulating than your most recent academic studies. You can also expect your compensation to be the lowest in this phase. Money is never unimportant, but it may be less important in the Aspiration Phase than it is later on.

The good news is that, in most entry-level positions, your work hours will be less intense than they are at later points in your career. (Of course there are exceptions, such as consulting, investment banking, law practice, and medical school.) You may also have more flexibility in terms of where you are willing to live. You may end up working in a major city like New York or Los Angeles. But don't be afraid to look for opportunities elsewhere, in a medium-size city or even in a foreign or emerging market, where the opportunities may be more plentiful and you can develop experiences that set you apart.

As most people move into the Promise Phase, the Career Triangle takes on a different shape, with job satisfaction and compensation overtaking lifestyle in terms of importance. Remember, the goal of this stage is to figure out your interests and what you're really good at and then to spend your time building a track

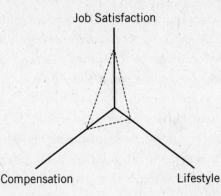

record of high-quality work in those areas of interest. Since the most important task in this phase is to become known as an outstanding contributor, you need to outwork your colleagues and competitors, often at the expense of your lifestyle.

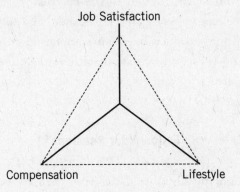

The Momentum Phase is when most people approach their peak financial value as a professional. In the Momentum Phase, it is both logical and appropriate to seek to maximize your current and long-term compensation. You are likely to be raising a family, so living in a place with good schools is paramount.

You know it's important to attend your children's soccer games, recitals, teacher conferences, PTA meetings, and other family events. You may need to balance the demands of your job against those of your partner or spouse's career.

Because of this, you may need to dial back your expectations for job satisfaction during the Momentum Phase. Of course, you'll want to work on challenges that will open new markets, businesses, and opportunities. But if you're in the Momentum Phase and pushing to become part of senior management, or to build a practice as a doctor, lawyer, engineer, or other professional, it is okay to recognize that, at least for now, your job is at least partially a means to an end rather than an end in and of itself.

As you move through to the Harvest, Encore, and Legacy phases of your career, you should be able to find the optimal balance between compensation, satisfaction, and lifestyle, consistent with your values, goals, and interests.

"Follow Your Passions"

Years ago, the advice to *follow your passions* was fresh, inspirational, and actionable. For many of you, I imagine, these words now strike a different chord.

In *Psychology Today*, San Francisco–based career coach Marty Nemko put forth why trying to "Do what you love!" and "Follow your passion!" is a risky strategy. Most people's passions center on travel, entertainment, fashion, sports, the creative arts, or cause-related issues, like education or the environment. As a result, jobs in these fields are hypercompetitive and tend not to pay very well. Governed by the laws of economics, employers in these fields usually pay those they hire below-market compensation, with the knowledge that such positions will have a line out the door of people willing to work for less money, or even for free.

> "If one more person tells me to follow my passions, I think I may get sick."
> **—NATE, TWENTY-TWO**

So how should you think about trying to align your interests with your career? One exercise to help you see which types of companies could be of interest to you is what I call the "kitchen table pile." Collect a bunch of business magazines and newspapers for a month or two, then sit down at the kitchen table and flip through them, tearing out any headlines or images that strike a chord. Don't overthink it or ask yourself why you're pulling out a particular piece. When you're done, separate your selections into piles, arranged by area of interest. Do any patterns emerge? If you are like most people, the thickest piles will be the kinds of things that trigger your enthusiasm. You can do the same exercise by bookmarking articles or blogs of interest over a few weeks and then organizing them into subfolders.

But perhaps a surer strategy for engaging your interests is to pursue them outside the workplace. After all, people have long pursued recreation and entertainment independent of their work responsibilities. People who love travel and adventure use their vacations to pursue those interests. Golfers, cyclists, paddleboarders, and lovers of other sports become weekend warriors. Food lovers pursue the culinary arts in the evenings after work, or on the weekends or holidays. There are endless schools, museums, charities, and other mission-driven organizations that you can support as a volunteer or board member.

Sometimes, if you are lucky and open to new experiences, an avocation manages to find its way back into your vocation. And it just may help your career in the process. When you are a singer, joining your company's band or a cappella group will help you to stand out from the crowd. When you are an environmentalist and organize your firm's community service day working to reclaim urban blight, you show your leadership and organization skills. And if your college golf career can help you cultivate a valuable mentor who loves talking (or playing) golf, you can find a basis of shared interest that makes it more natural for a senior person to invest in your success.

Next we'll do a deeper (and not necessarily politically correct) dive into the issue regarding the Career Triangle that might be causing the most anxiety for you right now: money.

3

WHAT ABOUT MONEY?

What single career issue gives you the greatest anxiety? If you're in your twenties and trying to picture what kind of life you want to live, the answer is probably money.

When we polled young professionals and top executives, we found that the two groups thought about money in dramatically different ways. For those already at the top, money was not the primary motivator; they cared more about having a job that was meaningful and that allowed them to have an impact on their company and the world. Those starting out in their careers, however, tended to be suspicious that there ever *would* be a day when money wasn't a major concern of theirs.

Eighty percent of young professionals reported that compensation was an "extremely important" factor in their happiness. When asked to identify the most successful person they knew, 85 percent strongly agreed or agreed with the statement "He/she makes a lot of money." The fact that fifteen other success attributes—such as how well liked they were, how well they handled adversity, the degree to which they were always learning, and whether they were physically fit—were cited less frequently shows just how important making money is to people in the early stages of their career.

"Here's what almost every recent college graduate is thinking: 'Do I look for a job in finance, an industry known to lead to high-paying careers? Or maybe high tech? Perhaps I just found my own company.'"

—RYAN, TWENTY-ONE

Andrew, an upperclassman in Syracuse University's Bandier School of Music, underscored that data. "I think more and more people think that being successful is defined by how much money you make," he said. "Money gives you freedom." Another student, Ryan, a rising senior at Cornell University, explained that his friends fall into two broad groups when they think about money and careers. "Some think strictly about money when consid-

ering jobs and future opportunities, even if they aren't *truly* interested in the work. Others think about being happy *and* making money. The former are the kinds who say, 'I want to work in investment banking for ten years, then go into private equity.' The latter say, 'I want to follow my dream to start and build something.' "

As the primary *objective* to enable you to live the life you want

As an important *component* in support of the work you want to do

In other words, you can decide that making money is your primary objective, as a means to pay off student debt and set you up to live the lifestyle you want. Or you can decide that making money is an important component and consideration in support of the work you want to do but not the only one—particularly in the early stages of your career.

Neither view is right or wrong. My goal here is to take the topic out from under the rug and allow you to think about it explicitly, for a change, with no value judgment. As it turns out, it's rare that you'll get the chance to speak on this subject in such terms. The fact is, regardless of how you *think* about money, it is usually not polite to *talk* about money. Unless you are extremely delicate about the subject, people will judge you when you talk about it, and they may in their minds label you greedy or overly driven by money. There is a time and place for talking about it, such as following a performance review or when you are negotiating for a new job (see chapter 13 Negotiating (or Not) to Get More

Money). Outside these contexts, it is generally wiser to reflect on money in the privacy of your own thoughts or with your closest confidants and to minimize the talk about it, other than acknowledging, when asked, that it is one of the factors that is important to you.

So, what if you find yourself in the first group, for whom making a lot of money is a primary objective?

The easiest path to making a lot of money is to choose a field that pays well. This sounds incredibly obvious. But it is also amazingly easy to overlook in your efforts to find a job, do well, and achieve all the other objectives as you start out. Ben Stein, a columnist for the *New York Times*, wrote a memorable article a number of years ago offering the advice to college freshmen that he wished he had received himself when he entered Columbia University in the early 1960s. "Over the years, I have seen it. Smart men and women in finance and corporate law always grow rich, or at least well-to-do. Incredibly smart men and women in short-story writing or anthropology or acting rarely do." The point is that you should go into whatever you do knowing that certain sectors pay much better than others.

Two words of caution if you're planning to go into a high-paying sector. First, your job might make you somewhat unhappy, or even miserable, in part because you'll probably be working in a highly competitive environment and in part because of the effects the job will have on your life outside work. Second, what may seem like a fail-safe profession today could be disrupted in the future by technology, outsourcing, a change in the marketplace, or a flood of new graduates flocking to your field. The more highly you are paid and the more specialized your skills, the more at risk you are to changes in your industry and in the economy at large. For example, a mortgage-backed derivatives trader who has spent ten years perfecting the arbitrage of yield spreads might find his skills not very transferable if the mortgage market craters or computerized trading renders his skills obsolete. The economy and the job market are always changing, and if you're working in a high-paying job sector it's important to plan ahead of trends and think constantly about how you can transform your experience into new potential.

What if you are in the other camp, where job satisfaction and lifestyle rate more highly than money on your Career Triangle at this stage in your life? How should you think about money?

Unless you fall into an unexpected inheritance, you probably will need to find creative ways to build financial independence. Develop the habit of thrift, learn to save wisely, and invest early, smartly, and consistently. Ben Stein said it much better than I could ever do. "If you're old enough to have sex," he wrote, "you're old enough to start saving and investing in a sensible way." In other words, thanks to the power of compound interest and the generally positive long-term performance of the stock market, a very sound financial strategy is to start saving and investing now.

$\ominus$

Let's now turn to the final topic of Part 1, the power of relationships and networks.

4

THE POWER OF RELATIONSHIPS
AND NETWORKS

In the previous chapter, I shared Ben Stein's advice about money. I want to begin here with another pearl of his wisdom that Stein wishes he had been given as a college freshman. "Success in life is so much about connections and whom you know," Stein says, "and so little about memorizing even the greatest of plays or knowing how to weigh the moon. There should be a special seminar in making and keeping connections."

Think of this chapter as that special seminar.

The old saying "It's not what you know but who you know" may well be hackneyed. But like most clichés it contains a strong element of truth. When it comes to finding a job and discovering ways to make progress in your career, there is simply no substitute for relationships and networks. According to the U.S. Bureau of Labor Statistics, 70 percent of all jobs are found through networking. So even if you're one of the 30 percent of people who beat the odds for your current job, the fact remains that employers fill the majority of positions with people they know or to whom they are personally referred.

"Is there life beyond online job postings? I have this feeling that for every posting there are actually five other jobs floating around that I'll never hear about because they go to friends."
—CHARLIE, TWENTY-TWO

In our survey of young professionals, more than half of the respondents reported having gotten their current job through networking. They were introduced to the hiring manager through a personal connection, were recruited by someone they knew, leveraged their university's alumni network, or were recommended to someone at the company by a family friend or mentor.

Networks and relationships are central to the process of landing a job. They're also essential to making sure you're successful and happy once you're *in* that job. Most of the things that you do in your professional life will depend on the cooperation of others. How you relate to those people will have a direct effect on your results. Even seemingly "nonrelationship" situations, like taking a class from a professor in college, volunteering in a company charity drive, or getting a ticket from a police officer, will be directly affected by your relationship skills. To achieve your goals, from securing the best job, to working on the most important projects, to earning a promotion, to building your reputation, you will need to gain the favor of people who are in a position to help or harm your cause.

Perhaps more importantly, the number one factor leading to happiness, according to our surveys and in-

NETWORKING YOUR WAY TO SUCCESS

How did you get your job?	Frequency
I applied to an opening online (job board, company website, LinkedIn, etc.)	22%
I had a personal connection with someone at the organization and they introduced me to the hiring manager	20%
I was recruited by someone with whom I had no prior connection	13%
I was recruited by someone I know	12%
I had a family friend or other personal connection introduce me to someone who works at the company	10%
I applied through a job fair/via on-campus recruiting	7%
I had an internship that led to a full-time job	6%
I successfully connected with someone with whom I had no prior relationship	5%
I reached out to an alum of my university and the alum was either the hiring manager or introduced me to the hiring manager	2%
I had a mentor who introduced me to someone who works at the company	2%

51% got jobs through networking

terviews, is *the quality of your relationships.* One hundred percent of the business leaders and 97 percent of the young professionals ranked relationships above their health, their personal impact, and their compensation in importance. It is imperative, consequently, to develop a relationship mind-set.

A Relationship Mind-Set

What do I mean when I talk about having a relationship mind-set?

First, remember that all business relationships are also personal relationships. The most common mistake people make when building relationships in their professional life, according to Keith Ferrazzi, author of the bestselling classic on networking *Never Eat Alone*, is treating business counterparts differently from personal friends. This approach not only makes for a lonely life at work; it also can work against you professionally, because genuine relationships lay the foundation for much of what happens in business, whether negotiations for a contract or job or opportunities to work on new kinds of projects.

Employers evaluate job applicants along two main dimensions: their experience and whether they're a "fit" for the company's culture. This means that, if you're interviewing for a job, the interviewer will be assessing you partly on the basis of personal relationships. Do they like you? Do they sense that they can trust you? Do they feel comfortable around you? The same is true when businesses award clients work, whether in advertising, technology, investments, consulting, accounting, or legal services.

So if personal relationships are so important, how can you build them with colleagues and clients? As it turns out, you shouldn't need to overthink this. You can build professional relationships in the same way that you make personal friends, by building trust through shared experience, commitment, honesty, and opening up your personal life (to an appropriate degree). As Ferrazzi explains, "Show them that besides being professional, you're human. Minimize the small talk and go into what really matters—your goals and dreams, your concerns and anxieties, your family situation and the business issues that keep you up at night. Don't think for a moment that they'll think less of you. In fact, usually the opposite happens." When you reveal important things about yourself, whether life experiences, thoughts, beliefs, or feelings, it deepens trust and commitment, thereby strengthening friendships and relationships.

Connections

Everyone knows that connections are important. Who your parents are, where you live, where you went to school, even whether you went to summer camp, these all influence how much access you have to influential people. The more connections you or your family have, the easier your access and the more readily you have the opportunity to build valuable relationships. But you don't have to be a Harvard Business School graduate or the daughter of a CEO to find connections.

> "Most students don't have mentors other than their parents, so those with parents in completely different sectors than what they want to do are often left out on a limb."
>
> **—SIAN, TWENTY-ONE**

By this point in your life, you know lots of people. You've been to high school and college, volunteered with organizations, played on sports teams, and developed shared interests and experiences with hundreds of people. Your family and friends, collectively, probably know thousands of people. You may not yet know the right people personally, but if you're creative, energetic, and positive, you will be able to find someone who knows someone who knows someone. Ask your aunt whom she knows on Wall Street. See if your high school math teacher, who went to Brown or Penn State, can connect you with a decision maker who turns out to have graduated in the same class. Go back to your university's career planning office and work with the advisers to build a list of prominent alumni in your field of interest. The more that you can adopt a relationship mind-set, the more opportunities will find a way to present themselves.

I Personally Dislike *Networking*

I really dislike the term *networking*. It's not that I have an aversion to meeting new people, building relationships, soliciting help, and proffering advice. I just find the term crass, bordering on sleazy. To me, *networking* connotes a giant cocktail party with inexpensive wine and hundreds of people I don't know all looking for a job. It involves a one-way street of exploiting others for your own gain. I much prefer the words and spirit behind the two-way street of *relationship building*.

That's not to say that networking is not important.

Very much the opposite. As Eric Barker writes in his weekly newsletter *Barking Up the Wrong Tree*, "Everyone needs to network. And I mean *everyone*." I cited research at the beginning of this chapter that shows that networking is essential to garnering the majority of jobs. But according to Eric, it also makes you more likely to be successful at your job, increase your salary, develop expertise based on valuable informal interactions, and be more creative.

> "Young people have the idea that everything is about connections. And not everyone necessarily has them, so it's easy sometimes to feel like you don't have a chance. People need to be told what networking is and how to do it."
>
> **—NICKI, TWENTY-THREE**

So what are the most relevant networking strategies for the aspiring young professional?

Here are my top three:

1. **Reconnect with old friends and reawaken dormant relationships.** Research suggests that people whom you used to be friends with but with whom you haven't been in recent touch can be even more helpful than people with whom you have a current, active friendship. Adam Grant, a professor at the Wharton School of Business and bestselling author of *Give and Take,* describes the power of what he calls weak ties. "Our closest contacts tend to know the same people and information as

we do. Weak ties travel in different circles and learn different things, so they can offer us more efficient access to novel information." So troll your extended Facebook friends. Follow up on the contacts suggested by LinkedIn, and be creative in trying to rekindle inactive relationships.

2. **Focus on your "super-connectors." These are the small number of friends and mentors through whom a disproportionate number of other friends and opportunities have come your way.** List your friends and key contacts, and trace how you first met them. Write the names of the people who introduced you, and you will probably see patterns emerging. Identify the brokers in your network and the networking practices you used to connect with them. Then focus your networking efforts—calls, e-mails, visits—on those people.

3. **Seek to help others.** To adapt John F. Kennedy's famous invocation, "Ask not what your colleague can do for you; ask what you can do for your colleague." The more that you can start thinking about how to help those who you meet, the more effective and rewarding relationship building and, yes, networking will be. When you have meetings and phone conversations, make sure you ask, "How can I help you?" as much as you ask for advice or help. After a meeting, rather than just sending a perfunctory thank-you note (but always send a thank-you note), share an idea or in-

sight or piece of news that links in some way to your conversation. This will show that you are thinking of them, which of course will make them that much more motivated to help you.

Build Your Career When You're Not Building Your Career

You don't need to be single-mindedly focused on your career to use networking to further your professional success. You can find plenty of legitimate opportunities outside work that will contribute to your professional relationships.

Consider the example of Amanda, a young professional who recently moved from the West Coast to the East Coast. A talented college tennis player, she wanted to join a tennis club in New York City. So she asked several of her friends and mentors, including her uncle, which clubs would be best and whether they knew anyone who could act as a sponsor. She was introduced to a board member of one of the clubs and went over to meet him for coffee. They chatted about tennis but also, naturally, about her career. Since she wasn't trying to "get anything" careerwise, the board member found it very natural and enjoyable to take an interest in what she was doing professionally. Together they went through the membership directory and built a list of potential endorsers for the club application process. Amanda had heard of one person and knew another very peripherally; the others only the board member knew. But she was able, over the next two months, to go about meeting five potential endorsers. Since the basis of the meetings was to talk about a legitimate area of mutual interest—tennis—it was easy for Amanda to schedule fifteen- or twenty-minute coffees with a handful of high-powered executives. Some of those meetings lasted an hour. Had she sought to set up these meetings for general networking or career advice purposes, they would have surely taken much longer to set. They would also have probably been more forced conversations at best, or never would have happened.

The success of this strategy in building relationships can perhaps best be explained by a principle referred to as "the Franklin Effect." Counterintuitive as it may sound, one proven way to spark a relationship with someone in power is to *ask* them for a small favor. In his book *59 Seconds: Think a Little, Change a Lot*, Richard Wiseman includes a passage from *The Autobiography of Benjamin Franklin* to illustrate a clever way Franklin managed to win over an enemy in the Pennsylvania state legislature:

> Having heard that he had in his library a certain very scarce and curious book, I wrote a note to him expressing my desire of perusing that book and requesting he would do me the favour of lending it to me for a few days. He sent it immediately and I returned it in about a week with another note expressing strongly my sense of the favour. When we next met in the House, he spoke to me (which he had never done before), and with great civility. And he ever after-

ward manifested a readiness to serve me on all occasions, so that we became great friends, and our friendship continued to his death.

Wiseman says that when someone does something for you they feel the need to justify it. Franklin explained his success as follows: "He that has once done you a kindness will be more ready to do you another than he whom you yourself have obliged."

Let me close this chapter with this thought. You might not have the ability to create a job or the demand for your services. You might not have the ability to control events that unfold around you. However, you do have significant control over a very valuable career strategy: building meaningful relationships that will both move you forward in your career and make your work life more successful and fulfilling.

Part 2

HOW TO *GET* THE JOB

5

TIME TO LAND SOME INTERVIEWS

> "The hardest part for me and my friends is getting that interview, finding a place to apply that could 1) fit your interests, 2) hopefully pay you a bit of money, and 3) consider you even if you are not in the 99th percentile of grades or experience."
>
> **—HARRY, TWENTY-ONE**

If you're in your final semester of college or have recently graduated, there's probably one question that you've come to dread more than any other: "So, what do you want to do with your life?"

This question is usually asked by parents, friends, or well-meaning adults who are trying to take an interest in you—but more often than not, the question just stresses you out. You feel embarrassed if you haven't locked down a job, and you feel judged if you don't have a concise, definite explanation for how you want to spend the next forty or fifty years.

At this point in your life, it truly is difficult to answer the question of what you want to do. You're not in a position to know the full range of jobs or even possible directions that might appeal to you, and you don't want to answer the question in a way that pegs you as being interested in only one or two lines of work. By this point, you've probably reflected on the Career Triangle and explored different fields through networking. But if you're indecisive about where you should start in your career and feel the need to get out and generate activity, now is the time to go out and land some interviews.

But before we begin, let's consider how you might respond if someone asks you what you want to do.

First, try to answer the question quickly, but not in a way that makes you seem indifferent or uninterested. Form a two-sentence elevator pitch that will give people an idea of who you are, what you're interested in, and what you've done in the past. The goal is that when the person you're speaking with comes across a potentially valuable connection or opportunity that could be right for you, your name will pop to mind.

Here are some possible answers to this question:

> *I'm interested in government work and am considering law school. I'm exploring paralegal opportunities and congressional internships to test this out.*
>
> *I love working in groups and am looking for a company that is known for collaboration and for doing much of its work in project teams.*
>
> *I'm passionate about the environment, so I'm looking at nonprofits that fight global warming and other environmental hazards.*
>
> *I've always loved the stock market, so I'm looking at a wide variety of opportunities in finance and investing.*

*I'm a competitive person. I want to find a
company that employs the smartest people
and has a demanding culture so that I can test
myself against the best.*

Find an answer that's specific enough to spark ideas
and thoughtful enough to create a good impression but
short enough to allow you to move on. Practice your
answer in front of the bathroom mirror until you can
recite it at will, then tuck it away for later use.

Now, let's turn to the specifics of how to go about
getting some interviews and searching for a job.

Create Your LinkedIn Profile

LinkedIn has become the de facto global platform
for job seekers and people who are serious about their
careers. In fact, in our survey 98 percent of people
reported having created a profile on the site. Most
employers will look at both your résumé and your
LinkedIn profile to get a feel for who you are and what
you've done. So you should make sure you have a presence there that's informative and compelling.

A good LinkedIn profile serves as an abbreviated
version of your résumé, detailing your education, professional affiliations, skills, internships, and work experience. Here are some tips to keep in mind when
creating your profile.

- In the work experience section, be specific when
  listing your job responsibilities and major accomplishments.

- Use the headline and summary spaces to explain your goals for your career.
- A profile picture is a must, as it livens up your page and shows your personality. Your picture should be recent and you should be alone, dressed as you naturally are but erring slightly on the side of looking professional.
- Remember to make your profile specific, concise, professional, and personal. An overworked profile can make you seem robotic, and one that is too long will discourage employers from reading about you.
- As a general rule, don't add people as connections unless you actually know them personally. Connections are for people with whom you've had legitimate conversations. The number of connections you have is not a status symbol.

Once you have created your LinkedIn profile, you can begin using it to explore job opportunities. While only a tiny percentage of young professionals report actually having gotten their job from a posting on LinkedIn, one in five have applied for a job they found on the site. It's always best to be given a warm introduction to someone you don't know, but still more than 40 percent have connected with someone they didn't know on LinkedIn to network in the hopes of being considered for a job. So, while you certainly can't count on LinkedIn to deliver job offers to your front door, it is an essential tool for managing your career and your professional connections.

Pursue Parallel Tracks

When you're beginning to set up interviews, your instinct may be to pursue one position or connection at a time, holding off on other opportunities until the current one has run its course. But, just as companies pursue multiple candidates for virtually every open position, it is appropriate, responsible, and to be expected that you will have multiple job leads developing in parallel. In fact, one question you can expect to hear in an interview or courtesy meeting is "Where else are you interviewing?" The more you have made inroads with a number of quality organizations, the more your potential connections will feel compelled to take you seriously. People are more inclined to want something if it's coveted by others, and the same holds true of you when you're interviewing for a job.

Build Your Target List

If you're working to open up parallel tracks that will lead to serious job opportunities, consider building a Target List of companies and organizations that interest you. It may sound like a basic step, but it can be one of the most helpful tools for organizing your job search and encouraging the kind of serendipity that can lead to an interview or a job offer.

Here's how you can build one.

Create a spreadsheet with columns for the basic facts of each organization: location, industry, number of employees, and links to any relevant websites. Large companies should be broken into multiple targets, as they frequently hire at the divisional level. For example, if you're pursuing a job in television, it's less useful to list Time Warner than it is to create separate entries for Warner Brothers, HBO, CNN, and Turner Broadcasting.

Visit the job boards on LinkedIn and each company's website, and add to your spreadsheet any job postings that border on your interests and experience. Make sure to include the requirements for the position and contact information for the recruiter.

Next, see if you know someone who works at the company. Even if none of your friends or close connections work there, you might be only one or two steps removed from someone who does. This is where LinkedIn can be particularly useful. When you search for an organization on LinkedIn, you will receive back a list of people affiliated with it, sorted by whether they are a "first," "second," or "third" connection. Make a column on your Target List for connections, where you can take notes on possible ways to make connections with companies on your wish list.

You can also find connections by reaching out to your contacts with a high-level summary of your interests and target organizations. You won't always get an introduction from someone in your immediate network, but there's no harm in asking. Remember the Franklin Effect. People enjoy helping friends and mutual connections, especially if you are respectful and positive in your approach. And you'll be surprised at how frequently the person you are talking with turns out to be in a position to help.

As you make more and more connections, use your spreadsheet as a to-do list and a running account of where things stand. Record all of the outreaches you've made or are planning to make, and take down any research steps or application deadlines.

It's important to exercise discipline with this exercise. You want to fill your Target List with useful information, but you don't want to cram it with so much data that you become overwhelmed. To keep your list from becoming unwieldy, try keeping it to a manageable number of companies. Your number might be fifteen, or it might be twenty-five, but beyond that your list risks becoming a time sink and a distraction from your job search.

See the next page for how an entry on your Target List might look.

Fish Where the Fish Are

When you're looking for a job, it's natural to feel that anyone who agrees to speak with you is doing you a favor. And if you're speaking to someone who doesn't have a job to offer, they probably *are* doing you a favor. But if you're speaking to a hiring manager or someone who's trying to fill an open position, you're in a different position altogether.

Let me underscore this point. Every hiring manager is trying to solve an urgent problem—"Who am I

Company **Location** **Size**	**Etsy** Brooklyn, NY 600 employees, $1.35 BN gross sales
Industry **Sector**	Consumer Internet
Websites	www.etsy.com www.etsy.com/careers/ www.etsy.com/careers/job/oGqAZfwp
Job Postings	**Quantitative User Experience Researcher** (Posted April 11 by Jane Chan, Technical Recruiter at Etsy) **Digital Marketing Specialist** (Posted March 30)
Connections	Uncle Jeff jeffsmith@gmail.com knows the VP HR, Ann Mason (LinkedIn contact)
Status	Applied for Quantitative User Experience Researcher posting on April 22 Scheduled to have telephone interview May 2 Asked Uncle Jeff for intro to VP HR for informational conversation and/or support for getting the Digital Marketing Specialist interview
Next Steps	Scheduled to meet Natalie for coffee— April 30 Buy and sell something on Etsy Read articles and watch CEO Chad Dickerson YouTube video May 2 phone interview Send cover letter and resumé for Digital Marketing Specialist

going to find to do this job? And will they be interested
once I find them?" If you happen to be a fit for the job
in question, you can approach the conversation with
confidence, because you can be the solution to that person's problem.

In doing your research, you might find that your target company doesn't have a position immediately available. More likely, the jobs listed on the organization's website call for more or different experience than you have at this moment. But don't be afraid to mention that position if you get the chance to speak with someone at the company. Even if you can't land that job now, it will provide a concrete starting point for the conversation, and it will help the other person to make sense of you in the context of their organization. For the Etsy positions on the Target List above, you might say, "I'd like to explore positions in Quantitative User Experience or Digital Marketing."

Inevitably, when you've built your Target List and used it to make connections and uncover serious job leads, you will find yourself looking at a message like this:

> If you're interested in joining the team at Etsy, please send a **cover letter** along with your **résumé** telling us why you'd be right for the position.

Now it's time for you to deploy the essential tools of the job application process.

Job Application Essentials—Your Résumé

> "I really want to make a difference, but I feel it's tough to communicate this in a cover letter and résumé."
> **—ANDREW, TWENTY-SIX**

There are countless articles, books, and online guides offering step-by-step instructions for writing a résumé, so I won't go into too much detail here. But I do want to emphasize a few broad guidelines:

- **Layout matters.** Format your résumé to look sharp and pleasing to the eye. Don't get too creative with unique designs. If you're applying to a company that values a good sense of design, you can supplement your résumé with a portfolio of your work or links to your online presence. But for your résumé, it's best to keep things simple.
- **Be concise and concrete** when highlighting your roles, experiences, and results. Include

two or three bullet points for each job listed, and be specific about your responsibilities and accomplishments, using numbers whenever possible to show results. Here are two examples of how you might describe a previous job:

- **Intern, Real Estate Development:** Scouted, documented, and presented new potential locations for retail stores, outlet stores, and warehousing. Played a critical role in the signing of a new lease for a warehouse in Orlando, Florida.
- **Studio Assistant, Commercial Photographer:** Assisted in approximately twenty commercial photo shoots in diverse settings with responsibility for preparation of sites, cameras, lenses, and lighting; supported execution of shoots and developing. Led follow-up with file management, archiving, and intellectual property clearances and served as liaison with photography and editorial staffs at various magazines including *Vogue*, *Vice*, and *Vanity Fair*.

- **Use action words** to describe your experience. You want the first word or two of each bullet point to give the reader an idea of what you did. Effective action words include *led, initiated, proposed, developed, determined, presented, conducted, mastered, researched, hired, grew*, etc.
- **Work memorable "icebreakers" into the personal section at the bottom of your resume.**

Employers often read résumés from the bottom up. You want to capture their imagination with a few memorable descriptors. Find something unique to you, such as *Climbed four of the Seven Summits by age twenty-two*; *Have hit three hole in ones in golf*; *Stand-up comedian*; or *Storm chaser: have gotten up close and personal with five tornadoes*. Don't leave your experiences or accomplishments like these off your résumé, as they might be the very thing that makes you stand out to the interviewer.

Job Application Essentials—Your Cover Letter

"What in God's name definitively makes a good cover letter? Questionable formulas aside, what are employers really looking for in the elusive cover letter? Personality? Competence? Mastery of the English language?
—ALEX, TWENTY-SEVEN

Let's make this simple: When you're writing a cover letter, your goal is to highlight your past experiences in a way that convinces the hiring manager to take the next step—bringing you in for an interview. A cover letter won't land you the job, but it *can* eliminate you from consideration. So be absolutely certain that your letter is concise, well written, cleanly formatted, and completely free of abbreviations, typos, and grammatical errors. Be patient in crafting your letter; it takes time to make sure you're expressing yourself in the right, professional tone.

Once you've written a strong cover letter for one job application, you can adapt it to other positions, depending on what language you find in each new job description. For example:

- If you're applying for an analyst position at a consulting firm, and the job description asks for qualifications like these:

  Skills in investigative research, close attention to detail, the ability to develop new conceptual frameworks, a strong intellectual point of view, exceptional work ethic, diligence and rigor, outstanding teamwork and collaboration, a goal-oriented personality, and international experience.

- You might write something like this in your cover letter:

  I believe that my strong academic record, the research and analysis skills demonstrated by my honors thesis, and time living in Argentina during college will allow me to perform the work of an analyst at a high level. In addition, my passion for working with fellow students and colleagues, as well as my membership on an NCAA DIII women's soccer team, underscores my excellence as a valued member of teams.

In a cover letter, you must convince your reader, in three paragraphs, that you are worth further attention. So choose your words carefully to establish your candidacy, illustrate your experience and personality, and say the most that you can within this framework.

Job Application Essentials—E-Mail Etiquette

"The number one question in my head is always, how do I draw the line between ambitious and annoying when contacting and pursuing potential employers?"
—JEFFREY, TWENTY-FIVE

In a world where most introductions happen over e-mail, it's probably not an overstatement to say that e-mail communication has become as important as— or even more important than—your skill at writing cover letters. With this in mind, here are my key tips for communicating effectively over e-mail:

- **Be incredibly responsive.** When someone introduces you to a new contact, it's imperative that you follow up immediately. If you had a phone conversation or an in-person interview, send a thank-you e-mail as soon as you get off the line or leave the building. Don't worry about coming across as desperate or creepy; this isn't a date. And even if an executive takes a few days to respond, or doesn't respond at all, it doesn't mean he or she won't be impressed if *you* respond immediately.
- **Tailor your e-mail to the situation.** When you've received an introduction to someone via e-mail, the goal of your response is to establish a connection and begin building a relationship. This isn't the time to ask for a job or internship; it's an opportunity to learn more about the per-

son and the company or industry. Then, once you've established an open channel of communication, you can share your goals and interests with more clarity and ask the person to connect you with their company's hiring manager.

- **Focus on the next step.** The goal of your e-mail is to get you to the next step, whether that is a phone call, a courtesy interview, or lunch. After you've been introduced to someone, your follow-up e-mail should be short, well written, and related to whatever was said previously. Here's an example of how you might follow up on a warm personal introduction:

  - Let's say your mentor or contact introduces you in this way:

    Dear Cliff,

    I hope you are looking forward to the summer and will get a well-deserved break. I'd like to ask you for a personal favor. Could I introduce you to an outstanding young woman who has a strong interest in e-commerce? Alyssa Greenberg is graduating from [school name] in a couple of months with a major in [field of study], and [company name] is one of her top choices. Her résumé is attached, but here are the highlights: blue-chip internship experience at Macy's, retail experience as a sales associate in CVS, and entrepreneurial experience setting up a store on eBay that sells Grateful

*Dead albums on vinyl. She would love to
see what's available at the company in
market research or digital marketing. She's a
fabulous people person, really smart, a great
team player, curious, persuasive, creative, and
an independent thinker ... she's just a great
young woman. I would be very appreciative
if she could get set up with the right person
for a conversation. Let me know!*

- You might try following up like this:

Dear Mr. [Cliff's Last Name],

*My name is Alyssa Greenberg, and I know
[mentor's full name] reached out to you over
the past weekend. I would be very interested
in learning about and potentially working for
[company name] and would love to connect. I
am free to talk at any time that is convenient
for you; and any help you could give me
would be truly appreciated. I look forward to
hearing back.*

All the best, Alyssa

- **Pay attention to the subject line.** The task
of your e-mail's subject line is to trigger an
impulse that causes the recipient to open the
e-mail. Your subject line should be enticing
and express who you are and what you are
writing about. Sometimes it is appropriate to
include your name, and other times your school
or connection or who referred you is the better
way to go. Here are some examples:

- Sarah Smythe Following Up on Ian McEwan's Introduction
- Indiana Student Interested in Learning More About the Marketing Services Industry
- ESPN Internship Application—Douglas Spector
- Middlebury Student Seeking 10 Minutes to Talk About Bain—Referral from Barry Rosenberg
- **When it comes to salutations, err on the side of formality.** Unless you are e-mailing a close friend or family friend who has previously asked that you use his or her first name, always use Mr. or Ms. Even if the recipient signs his or her response with a first name, continue using Mr. or Ms. for at least the first two or three exchanges.

One caveat is that the norms for salutations vary across different countries and industries. In America, even the most senior executives tend to be more comfortable using their first names than are people from Germany, France, Japan, the United Kingdom, and elsewhere in the world. Likewise, a veteran CEO of a manufacturing company is likely to prefer to be addressed in a different way than the thirty-two-year-old founder of a tech start-up. When in doubt, lean toward formality in salutations until your counterpart requests otherwise.

- **Begin by explaining the occasion for your message.** The first line of your e-mail will

vary, depending on whether you're address-
ing someone from your immediate network
or someone to whom you've been introduced.
But no matter the situation, your opening line
should explain why you're contacting the recipient. You may often open up by saying something along the lines of the following:

- No Prior Contact: I hope this note reaches
  you in high spirits and good health. I am
  reaching out to you in the hope of learning more about the medical diagnostics
  industry in general and Medtronic specifically.

- Referral: I hope you are having a great
  weekend and that this doesn't catch you
  at an inconvenient time. I was speaking
  with my uncle Ken, and he explained
  to me that you direct your firm's retail
  practice. I am very interested in explor-
  ing a career in retail and fashion, and I
  believe you would be the perfect person
  to talk to.

- One Prior Contact: Thanks again for our
  conversation a couple of weeks ago. I
  followed up as you suggested and found
  three or four specific target companies
  with potentially relevant positions to apply to. Could we connect on the phone for
  seven to ten minutes so I can get your input about these opportunities?

- **Keep it short.** Most people don't have the time or attention span to read an e-mail that's longer than ten lines. Assume that the recipient will be reading it on his or her smartphone (while multitasking), so make it snappy, establishing who you are and what you want in the first two sentences. Write your e-mail in at least 11- or 12-point font so that the reader doesn't have to put on his or her reading glasses.

> "Sometimes I just don't hear back. It's such a drag."
> —CONRAD, TWENTY-ONE

- **Put yourself in the recipient's shoes, and always keep your cool.** Chances are, you will be reaching out to people who are very busy. Unread e-mails don't bring them joy; they make them anxious, and your e-mail will be adding to the count. People are often stressed when responding to e-mail. So if you haven't heard back from someone, or if they've sent you a less-than-warm response, it doesn't mean that they dislike you or think you're not good enough. It doesn't even mean the conversation is over. More often than not, the recipient is just hesitant to add an unexpected task to the pile. Don't be afraid to continue reaching out. Find the right frequency—perhaps once every two weeks—until your contact replies with a next step or tells you he or she isn't interested. Even

then, don't necessarily cross people or companies off your Target List. Just thank them for
their time and move them to your list's inactive section. You might try them again in a few
months, or they might become important for
you years later in your career. An e-mail can
be forwarded in an instant, so don't jeopardize
your relationships and your network by writing something in the heat of the moment that
will come back to haunt you.

"I don't want preferential treatment, but even an
e-mail rejection would be nice. This whole 'If you do not
hear back from us, your application is unsuccessful' is
utter rubbish. A little courtesy would go a long way."
—TORI, TWENTY-ONE

Keep Calm and Carry On

"Getting a job you want takes intense focus, and the
modern world is so distracting that you can easily fool
yourself into a tepid existence where you are neither
pursuing something nor letting your dream die."
—OLIVIA, TWENTY-FIVE

The work of securing interviews and applying for jobs
is a painstaking and circuitous process. There will
be times when you can't generate promising leads or
when people don't respond to your e-mails. There will
be times when promising opportunities turn out to be
dead ends, and the search almost always lasts longer

than you expect. But there's one way to make a job search at least somewhat rewarding: start treating the *process itself* as if it were a job.

The more you view your search as a rare opportunity to learn about companies, sectors, positions, and people, the more interesting it will be, and the more you will grow from the process. Even when your circumstances become discouraging—and there's a good chance they will—stay resolute, confident, and positive. Or, as articulated by the World War II advertising campaign designed to keep the peace within the United Kingdom (and today gracing coffee mugs, tote bags, and mouse pads everywhere), Keep Calm and Carry On.

OVERCOMING THE PERMISSION PARADOX: YOU CAN'T GET THE JOB WITHOUT EXPERIENCE, BUT YOU CAN'T GET EXPERIENCE WITHOUT THE JOB

The Permission Paradox is the catch-22 that confronts every job seeker and person trying to move forward in his or her career. All too often, *You can't get the job without the experience, but you can't get the experience without the job.* You will run into this frustrating dilemma at every point of your professional life, as you work to get promoted, change industries or sectors, or move from one functional role to another. And the Permission Paradox is particularly challenging when you're in the Aspiration Phase and are trying to land your first job.

It is frustrating because, since you don't have a résumé packed with big-time jobs and dazzling accomplishments, there's no way for you to demonstrate definitively that you deserve a job in the Aspiration Phase. But you know you could deliver if only someone would give you the chance. Sometimes it just takes time for that chance to arrive, but it's easy to become bitter or disillusioned as you search for that one person who's willing to give you your first shot.

The good news is that the Permission Paradox is not an iron law. Remember, early in your career, employers value you more on the basis of your potential than on the basis of your experience. If you demonstrate enthusiasm, a good attitude, strong communications skills, curiosity, willingness to learn, and knowledge of your role, you're further along than you might think. The trick, however, is to show potential while also finding ways to at least hint at, if not demonstrate, your experience.

Here are six specific strategies for overcoming the Permission Paradox.

Six Ways to Break the Permission Paradox

1. **Build Credentials.** Consider obtaining a professional certification or taking an online course that will teach you a marketable skill. For example, one of the most desired skills in today's economy is computer programming. The U.S. Bureau of Labor Statistics projects that by 2020 there won't be enough computer science graduates to fill the growing number of jobs in the field. Even today, nearly 15 percent of Google's programmers don't have a *college* degree, and companies outside the tech world are coming to see programming as a skill to be valued in any employee. If you think the companies you're interested in might value coding skills, consider taking an online course from a site like Codecademy, which can help you develop proficiency in a period of months. That one extra skill might just be the factor that helps you get your foot in the door for a job.

Even if you're not interested in coding, chances are there are valuable hard skills that you can learn in your spare time. For example, many colleges offer six-week summer courses on business and finance; for most other disciplines, from health care to aviation, there are programs offering credentials. Christie's auction house, for example, has postgraduate programs in the business of art. The time and cost of building credentials might seem daunting, especially if you are struggling to pay off student loans. But many of these professional development courses are inexpensive, and some, such as Coursera, are free.

2. **Get Creative.** Laura Chambers leads a team at eBay tasked with recruiting new hires and ensuring that eBay's interns and recent hires have a positive experience. Laura advises new graduates to think outside the box when trying to break into the company of their choice. "If you want to work at eBay," she says, "start a small business buying and selling on eBay, or using PayPal, and be prepared to talk about the pros and cons of that experience." Consider creating a few videos or blog posts to share what you learned. It doesn't have to cost much, other than your time and energy, but it will enable you to talk about your experience, not just your potential, when interviewing for a job.

3. **Don't Be Afraid to Start at the Bottom.** If you are a college graduate, you may be overqualified for many entry-level jobs. But as Lao Tzu famously said, "The journey of a thousand miles begins with one step."

Chad Dickerson, CEO of Etsy.com, suggests that working on a company's support team—in a role like executive assistant, cashier, or customer service representative—is often the best way to get your foot in the door and gain valuable experience. "A number of Etsy's support people have learned our business really well," he said. "They turned into very capable product managers." Chad admits that he favors this approach in part because it worked for him. "In 1993, I took the lowest-paid clerical job at a newspaper in Raleigh, North Carolina, and it happened to be the first daily newspaper in the United States to go online. I ended up learning how to build websites just by being there!"

If you want to work in a sector that serves large numbers of people—technology, financial services, retail, hospitality, health care, or politics—starting off at the point of customer interaction will give you a unique view of what's really going on in the market, and this experience will serve you well when you get the chance to work in the corporate office.

4. **Barter.** If you don't have a job, chances are you do have something else of value: *time*. If you use your time creatively, you might be able to barter your way past the Permission Paradox.

Consider the case of Sarah, a recent college graduate who networked her way to an informational interview with an executive at a real estate firm. Midway through the conversation, Sarah noticed that the executive seemed overwhelmed, and it gave her an idea. "You seem incredibly stretched right now," she said. "What would you do to grow your business *if you had an extra day in your week?*" This stopped the executive in his tracks. He paused for a moment before telling Sarah that, if he had the time, he would do an in-depth study to help his company target young people in the urban rental market. She offered to do that study for him, explaining that the skills in writing and analysis that she had developed for her thesis would help her to execute this project. The executive took up the offer and even decided to pay Sarah $15 an hour for her work.

In a few weeks, Sarah presented her findings. The executive was blown away by the quality of her report and the creativity with which she packaged her ideas. He offered her a job on the spot as a market researcher in the firm. Sarah broke the Permission Paradox by turning an informational interview into a try-before-you-buy opportunity for the executive. If you pay close attention to the needs of the people you're connecting with, you might be able to barter your way into a good job.

5. **Reimagine Your Experience.** When applying for an entry-level position, you may find that you just don't have the experience the employer is looking for. At this point, you can throw in the towel and move on to the next company, or you can try to reimagine your experience in a way that gives you a shot at the very opening that sparked your interest.

Here's how one recent graduate did just that. James was interested in an entry-level position at a food company, but the job posting listed "experience in project management" as a requirement for candidates. James was discouraged because he didn't have a job on his résumé that demonstrated that skill. But in talking with a friend, he realized that he did in fact have the experience the company was looking for—he just needed to describe it in a different way.

James told the story of how, as a geography major

who loved to travel, he worked with a group of friends to "project manage" a three-week trek across eastern Europe. He researched itineraries, found the lowest fares and cheapest hostels, booked the reservations, and acted as "treasurer" for the journey. By including this story in his cover letter, James was able to demonstrate that he did in fact have the capabilities that the food company was looking for—even though the experience had absolutely nothing to do with a formal job.

The point is, you probably have more job-relevant experience than you think. You might just need to re-imagine your experience in a way that fits the requirements of the position.

6. **Get an Internship.** More than half of the respondents in our survey reported having taken an internship at some point. The most common timing was between their junior and senior years of college, and many people's internships turned into full-time jobs upon graduation. But job placement, it turns out, does not have to be the primary goal of an internship. On the basis of our survey, the most important—and common—role of an internship is helping you to break the Permission Paradox.

Only 5 percent of young professionals in our survey got their full-time jobs *directly* from an internship. For the other 95 percent, internships played a different, but still important, role: helping them gain on-the-job experience and exposure to different environments. An internship should also offer you the chance to network and build relationships that can later be leveraged in your search for a full-time job.

Postgraduate internships aren't as common as college

internships, but they are becoming more and more of a norm. Of the people in our survey who reported having taken an internship, one in three disclosed that the internship took place after they graduated from college. Sometimes companies hire graduates as paid interns to test them out before offering full-time jobs. Other times, new graduates offer up their services as an unpaid intern, hoping that the quality of their work will earn them a full-time offer. There is no magic for making ends meet financially if you take a low-paid or unpaid internship after graduating from college. Some recently graduated interns are fortunate to be able to rely on their families for a period of time, while many others have to find paying jobs at night or on weekends as waiters or bartenders, or in retail to fit around their internships.

What defines a good internship experience? Among our young professionals, 90 percent cited *learning* and *fun* as the most important factors. Following closely behind were the opportunities to be challenged and to build strong relationships.

—⊖—

No matter which of the six strategies you end up using, I hope this chapter has helped you see that the Permission Paradox doesn't have to block you from good opportunities. In one way or another, every person who has landed a job has broken the stranglehold of the Permission Paradox. If you are creative, persistent, curious, enthusiastic, and show you have potential, you'll be surprised at how many doors you can open.

YOU'VE STUDIED LIBERAL ARTS, NOW WHAT?

If you majored in electrical engineering or computer science, you can skip this chapter. If you studied accounting, pre-med, construction management, finance, petroleum engineering, agriculture, pharmacy, or nursing, you may find this section interesting but superfluous. However, if you're studying the humanities or have recently graduated with a liberal arts degree, these pages are dedicated to you.[1]

---

[1] Full disclosure, I am personally biased in favor of the humanities in particular. I studied economics with four years of romance lan-

You are about to read some statistics that might stress you out. But fear not: there is a case for optimism.

If you majored in a field like history, English, political science, anthropology, music, art history, geography, or women's studies, the $64,000-a-year question is, how can you take your degree and compete in the job market? This question is becoming more difficult to answer today, in a time when liberal arts majors are more likely to be unemployed, underemployed, or less well compensated than their counterparts who studied engineering, computer science, or business.[2]

---

guages, I served as a trustee of my alma mater, Vassar College, for twelve years, and I've also been on the board of Wesleyan University, where my two sons graduated, for the past five years.

[2] In 2010, the humanities, which comprise "the most liberal of the liberal arts" programs, accounted for 17 percent of the 1.65 million bachelor's degrees awarded in the United States, according to the *Chronicle of Higher Education*. Sixty percent of liberal arts and communications majors were underemployed in the 2009 to 2011 period, according to *Bloomberg Businessweek*. Social sciences, humanities, and "general studies and other" all had unemployment rates above 9 percent, and almost 24 percent of humanities majors held four or more jobs after graduation—far more than in any other field. By contrast, three-quarters of engineering, education, and health care students held jobs matching their skills. In 2012, 95 percent of college graduates with computer science degrees had a job, and the rate of employment among business majors was nearly as high, at 94 percent. Not only were they more gainfully employed, but their pay was significantly higher than that of humanities ma-

The reality is that if you're studying the humanities, you will need to work harder, be more creative, and draw on your unique skills and strengths to land an ideal job. This is why many students enter the academic world with a plan for building credentials, whether by double-majoring in a technical field or by taking skill-focused elective courses that will enhance their résumés. In fact, at many liberal arts colleges, computer science and other branches of engineering, as well as math and sciences, are among the most popular majors. So the data are more complicated than suggested by a simple bifurcation between liberal arts and vocational instruction.

Personally, I am convinced that a liberal arts education—with small-size classroom discussions facilitated by dedicated professors who love to teach, taking place in a shared residential living and learning environment—will prove invaluable in your career. The skills that are forged through this experience, like critical thinking, information synthesis, problem solving, and effective communications, will put you in good stead. That is, once you get the chance to apply them.

But the question still stands: How can you justify paying $60,000 a year for a liberal arts degree when it's becoming less likely that the degree will land you a decent-paying job upon graduating?

---

jors. According to the Department of Education, in 2012, engineering and computer science graduates from the years 2007 and 2008 had median annual salaries of over $60,000, whereas humanities and social sciences graduates from the same years had median salaries of $40,000 or less.

Before moving on to strategies and solutions, let me share some historical context. This question, it turns out, isn't a new one. According to Michael Roth, president of Wesleyan University and author of *Beyond the University,* "The failure of professors to teach their students how to navigate in the real world has been a staple of criticism of colleges in America since the founding of Harvard in 1636." Throughout most of American history, college was seen as something only rich families could provide their children—more specifically, their sons. In the early and mid-1800s, people were concerned as to whether a broad-based education would adequately prepare students for the economic and technological changes that were sweeping society. Sound familiar? In that era, the changes were being brought about by the industrial revolution, assembly-line manufacturing, transoceanic shipping, and the rise of the railroad.

The liberal arts withstood those challenges, and they can withstand the challenges that face them today, provided that employers continue to need people trained in inquiry, analysis, communications, problem solving, and self-discovery. Of course, while that notion of future value is nice, it does not solve the problem of finding a job and getting a paycheck today. Nor does it ignore the fact that the first step for a humanities graduate is often more difficult to get right.

"Many students are told they're perfect for jobs and then get rejected. They generally don't receive any feedback, so they don't know why they were rejected. Searching for a job is a new model from academia, where students get instant and consistent evaluations. The new system is incredibly stressful."

—DAN, TWENTY-ONE

So, what to do if you're a liberal arts major?

To help answer this question, I interviewed a cross section of business leaders and HR officers in industries like technology, finance, social media, entertainment, not-for-profit, and government. I posed each person this question:

> If you were choosing between a candidate with a technical degree and a liberal arts major, what would the liberal arts student need to do in order to win out?

On the basis of leaders' responses to this question, liberal arts graduates have plenty of reason to be optimistic that they can win entry-level jobs and launch careers that are meaningful and successful.

Clara Shih, a Stanford graduate who founded Hearsay Social, an enterprise software company, and serves on the board of Starbucks, estimates that 30 percent of her employees majored in the liberal arts. "Some of the more technical roles do require specific technical training," she says. "But generally, we look for the willingness and ability to learn fast, a strong work ethic, and cultural fit."

Clara tries to hire people who are well-rounded, whether they were trained in the humanities or in technology. "Just as we appreciate well-rounded technical students who read Shakespeare and Tolstoy, liberal arts students can become more interesting candidates by dabbling in technology, say by taking introductory programming classes and building apps on the side." In other words, your degree matters, but what really counts is the extent to which you complement your major with elective courses and find ways to build hard skills in your spare time.

Even in finance and private equity, there is hope for liberal arts students. Jeff Citrin, co-managing principal of Square Mile Capital, a leading real estate private equity firm, told me that one of his firm's very best junior employees was a philosophy major who worked for a large investment bank for two years following graduation. "This associate has incredible poise, the ability to communicate, and solve problems," he said. Jeff likes to hire candidates who have had a grounding in humanities but have an aptitude for finance and who have picked up some technical skills on the side. "We put our serious candidates through deep case studies to see how their minds work and how they structure problems." The young man showed amazing aptitude and they hired him.

Jay Walker, who founded Priceline.com and holds 710 patents in the United States and internationally, says, "I have often been forced to choose between hiring somebody who is technically trained and somebody who is much more general in their background. I often choose the generalist over the technician."

However, Jay admits, this preference is not shared by every employer. "It's important to recognize that a liberal arts education is not a commercial credential," he says. "The market will always pay for credentials, whether an engineering degree, a medical degree, or a law degree. If you want to work in a field that worships credentials, then you have to get credentials— simple as that. It's just not productive to go against that reality."

But fields like finance and technology aren't the only industries in which liberal arts students can find success. Alec Ross is a perfect example of this. After graduating from Northwestern University in 1994 with a history degree, Alec joined Teach for America and later went on to become Hillary Clinton's senior adviser for innovation. In that capacity, Alec led a team in the U.S. State Department that helped people around the world use technology and social media to pursue democracy, aid in disaster response, and respond to regional conflicts. During his two years in the State Department Alec traveled to over 150 countries and had teams on the ground in some of the most volatile areas training and partnering with locals to support America's diplomatic goals in political reform and recovery from natural disaster.

Alec looks for three qualities when hiring someone with a liberal arts background:

1. *Intellectual horsepower.* "I would want to be convinced that they had superior processing power so that if they were faced with highly technical problems to solve, they would have

the ability to either solve it themselves or to draw on the expertise of others to develop a solution."

2. *Curiosity and a commitment to lifelong learning.* "It is less important what specific degree a graduate has than his or her demonstrated interest and aptitude for learning across fields. The idea that an undergraduate or graduate degree is the end of one's education—formal or informal—is over."

3. *Cultural/linguistic fluency.* "If someone is not 'fluent' in a technical language, e.g., computer science, then I would hope that they would be fluent in at least one other language and culture that is relevant to the expansion of my business. A liberal arts major who is fluent in Brazilian Portuguese and knows her or his way around São Paulo could add real value to my enterprise."

Concrete Advice for Liberal Arts Students and Graduates

Now that you have the background and context for how to leverage your liberal arts education, it's time to get practical. Here are six pieces of advice that when coupled with the other strategies and tactics in *The Career Playbook* should put you in good stead.

1. **Know Your Skills and What You Want to Do.** Don't be the kind of liberal arts student

who can't communicate what they're good at and what they want to do. Be prepared to connect the strengths you demonstrated in school to a skill that employers will value. A hiring company won't make the effort to solve that problem for you. For example, if you're a first-rate researcher who enjoyed studying complex and intricate macroeconomic issues, you might consider working in market research or product development.

2. **Become Skilled in Tomorrow's Disciplines.** Alec Ross suggests that you "commit to gaining a foothold in the fields that will propel tomorrow's economy," including big data, analytics, genomics, cyber, and machine-learning/robotics. "Demonstrate to employers that you aren't just a star-gazing poet" by departing from your comfort zone and taking classes outside a traditional liberal arts focus. "I like it when a comp lit major tells me that he took an intro to programming class because both comp lit and programming are rooted in 'language' and its structures." If you supplement your humanities studies with work in tech and engineering disciplines, it will put you on even footing with graduates from more preprofessional programs. And if you do this while also taking advantage of your broad liberal arts education, you might even find yourself ahead.

3. **Meet with Career Services and Alumni Relations.** Chances are, your career services and

alumni relations offices are working hard to help connect students with internships and entry-level jobs. Solicit their advice early and often in your undergraduate days. Enroll in programs aimed at helping students and alumni succeed in their job search. Talk with the career center about the types of jobs and companies that interest you, and then follow any leads they connect you with.

Appendix B details many of the things that college career services and alumni relations offices are doing to support your success—both because they care about you and as a matter of their own survival. Think of it this way: your school's career department needs examples they can point to when trying to talk about how successful they've been. Why not make yourself one of those success stories?

4. **Be Creative About Getting Your Foot in the Door.** Networking is important for everyone, but it is especially important for liberal arts students. This is because liberal arts majors graduate with fewer clear credentials that employers can rely on when making hiring decisions. Laura Chambers, who runs eBay's program for new employees, says that any time a position comes up that's appropriate for a liberal arts major, the company receives thousands of applications. In a situation like this, it is important to take advantage of any connections you have to find someone who can

introduce you to someone else at the company. Chambers says, "Finding a way to leverage any connections will ensure you get noticed among the crowd."

5. **Think Globally.** Alec Ross advises liberal arts majors to consider working outside the traditional business hubs in the United States or western Europe. "Today's frontier economies are tomorrow's developing economies, and today's developing economies are tomorrow's *developed* economies." Graduates can position themselves for the long term if they're willing to sweat it out in a frontier economy while their friends are living it up in New York City, San Francisco, and London.

6. **Consider Sales.** If you are persuasive and enjoy being around people, your liberal arts background can help you become a strong performer in sales. "No good salesperson is unemployed," Jay Walker says. "Sales is the best job in the world if you like people, can communicate and synthesize well, and are skilled at solving other people's problems. The fact is, nothing happens in the world without sales. Give me any field, and I'll show you how, without sales, there is no forward momentum. Even scientists have to sell to get their funding. There is never a recession in sales."

If you're a liberal arts student, I hope these pages have helped you to breathe more easily. Your education has taught you plenty of valuable, marketable skills, and if you work creatively to apply them, you will be able to weather the storms of an ever-changing job market.

Now, let's get even more practical by digging into the moment of truth for any job search: the interview.

THE ART OF THE INTERVIEW

When you're looking for a job that will launch your career, the job interview is your moment of truth. You will be interviewing, in one form or another, throughout the entire course of your career, and it's a skill you need to develop as time goes on. But it's never too soon to learn everything you can about the art of the interview.

I have conducted thousands and thousands of interviews in my career, and I've distilled from that experience five key pieces of advice. If you follow these five tips, I have every confidence that you will stand out from the pack and put yourself in prime position to earn the job you covet.

Interview Tip #1: Don't Just Answer Questions, Tell a Narrative

Because of the way most interviews are structured—in question-and-answer format—you might think your task as the interviewee is to listen carefully to each question and come up with a reply that's thorough and earnest. That's exactly how most people approach the process—but it's actually less than ideal. The best way to ace an interview is to tell a *story* by connecting your answers to one another in a way that gives the interviewer a memorable, three-dimensional picture of who you are.

Take, for example, a sociology major who was interviewing for an entry-level job in digital media, targeting advertising sales. When prepping for the question "What are your greatest strengths and weaknesses?", he came up with this planned response:

> *I'm a people person with strong research and analysis skills, and I'm absolutely passionate about media. As to my weaknesses, I don't have experience in coding or the technical aspects of your product.*

That's a solid answer, but I told him he could do better. Here's what we came up with:

> *My greatest strengths are that I'm a highly creative person who builds powerful relationships and works well with others. For example, when I was researching my sociology honors thesis, I*

had to go into low-income public housing projects and establish trust with the residents so I could capture and relate their family stories in the project. From my time spent playing lacrosse, from youth all the way through four years of college, I have come to learn not only that it's fun to be on a team but that you can accomplish things through teamwork that simply cannot be replicated by working alone. My weakness is that I haven't yet had training in coding—but if I were to join your company, I would find a way to learn.

Same guy, same experience, different narrative. Which answer would you buy?

Interview Tip #2: Avoid the Trap in "Do You Have Any Questions for Me?"

When the interviewer asks, "Do you have any questions for me?" don't be fooled. This is *not* the moment to relax or think that the interviewer is just being polite or trying to wrap up the meeting. This is your chance to show that you've done your homework on the company and the position and that you're a savvy candidate who actually knows that this is one of the most important parts of the interview.

The *worst* possible answer to this question is "No, thanks, I think I have everything I need." If you don't have any questions, the interviewer will write you off as someone who isn't hungry and isn't interested in the organization. So prepare for this question ahead of time, and be ready to ask a series of questions that support your narrative.

Assuming you've done your homework, it is acceptable—and actually to your advantage—to ask tough questions about the company's strategy and culture. Demonstrate that you're thoughtful and well informed, but don't cross the line into being insulting or overly personal.

Here are just a few examples of the kind of questions you might ask:

About the Culture

How would you describe the kinds of people who thrive in the company versus those who don't?

In my first job, the company culture was all about collaboration, teamwork, and never using the word I; in my second, the people who stood out were individual stars. Where does your organization fall on that spectrum?

About the Position

What would success look like in this job? If I were offered this position, what would I need to accomplish in the next year for you to look back and say, "What an amazing year you've had!"?

About the Company

In the most recent earnings call, the chief financial officer said that the company is projecting flat revenue for the year, even though the market is growing by double digits. Are you concerned about the company's strategy?

How do your salespeople pitch the company, relative to your biggest competitor? For example, when I was an intern at ESPN, everyone always talked about how we were the dominant player—"The Worldwide Leader in Sports." We didn't always have the largest audience in television, but it was a passionate one, and we knew that was our greatest strength when pitching clients.

About the Interviewer

Could you tell me about your story? How did you find your way to the company? How does it compare to your prior organization? What have you enjoyed most, and what has been most frustrating?

Remember: people love to be asked about themselves. Ideally, you will know ahead of time the name of your interviewer, and you can research that person on Google and LinkedIn to form questions about his or her individual career path and professional achievements.

Questions of General Advice

In the retail field, what are the advantages and disadvantages of starting out on the sales floor versus starting at the company headquarters?

How often do employees start in one department of the company and move into another? What is the process for that to happen?

I love international cultures and am at a point in my life where I am completely mobile geographically.

*What are the opportunities for working in different
locations as one proves oneself within the organization? How does the company go about creating business leaders with global experience?*

Warning: In an interview, bad questions do exist!
Try not to ask questions about facts that are readily
available in the public domain. Even if you're genuinely interested to know the answer, these kinds
of questions risk making it look as if you haven't
done your homework. A good rule of thumb is that
if you can get an answer from a Google search, you
should already know it ahead of the interview.

Your goal is for the interviewer to describe you later
as being "very sharp and asking great questions." Asking great questions is one of the most sure-fire ways to
succeed in an interview and ultimately get the job.

Interview Tip #3: How to Compete When
You're at a Disadvantage

This relates to the broader topic covered in the previous
chapter—how to compete if you've studied liberal arts
and humanities—but it applies to everyone. No matter
what you studied or what your experience has been to
date, there will be times in your career when you will
be competing against candidates who have more im-
pressive credentials, training, and experience than you.
Even if they do, it doesn't mean that you can't turn your
position to an advantage.

I was speaking with the father of an art history major who was interviewing for positions in investment banking. The dad was worried and said, "I have no idea how to advise my son when he's asked by the interviewer, 'Why should I hire an art history major when I could hire a finance major instead?' "

That question cuts to the heart of the broader question about the liberal arts. In today's economy, which puts such a premium on technical skills and specialization, it is easy to take a defeatist attitude and concede that all of the good corporate jobs will go to engineers or MBAs.

But there's another way to look at the issue, a way that plays to the strengths of liberal arts students. Here's how that art history major might answer the investment banker's question:

> There are three reasons you should hire me over a finance major: First, financial modeling, while obviously an important skill in investment banking, is becoming a commodity. With spreadsheets and other modeling tools, any analyst can do these basics. I've studied these on my own, and if I have the opportunity to join your firm, I will quickly be able to learn how to do the necessary financial analysis. Second, my work in art history is actually excellent training for seeing patterns across markets, which is how I believe value is really added in investment banking. I've had to learn about history, government, culture, architecture, and psychology in addition to art. With my experience in this kind of cross-disciplinary

investigation, I can help the firm search for new investment opportunities. Third, investment banking is a client service business, and your firm's clients surely have interests beyond the deal and business. Thanks to my work in art history and a broad range of other subjects, I will be able to engage with senior-level clients in areas that will prove memorable to them and help the firm build meaningful relationships.

The point here is that you can turn apparent disadvantages into points of distinction. It takes courage and gumption to do this, but I promise that it will make you memorable and help the interviewer to recognize your potential.

Interview Tip #4: Clarity Gets the Job

At the most senior levels in business, the most successful candidates (often for CEO positions) are those who are able to:

1. Explain the key competitive dynamics in the industry (i.e., what is driving change, who is winning, who is losing, and why).

2. Clearly describe what the company should do to thrive (i.e., what the top priorities should be, what strategies should be pursued, and what acquisitions should be considered).

3. Present a sound and detailed strategy for organizing the company in a way that helps it move forward decisively and effectively (i.e.,

which positions should report directly to the CEO, which functions should be centralized or pushed into the business units, and how to align incentive systems to reward the desired behaviors).

The least successful candidates are, by stark contrast, muddled in their thinking, generic in their diagnoses, unclear about the company's priorities, and rambling when they describe which strategies they think the company should pursue.

The same principle holds true when you're interviewing for a job further down the totem pole. You probably won't be asked to give an overview of a company's strategic positioning when you're interviewing for an entry-level job. But if you can demonstrate to your interviewer that you are a clear thinker who expresses yourself coherently, you will put yourself ahead of the crowd.

Interview Tip #5: Communicate with Confidence

Some people are effective communicators in a normal setting, but as soon as they sit down for an interview they freeze up and lose their cool. They avoid eye contact. They fall into using verbal crutches, like "you know" or "I mean." Their feet start tapping, and their hands move as if they're disconnected from their brain.

Your strengths as a job candidate can be obscured—or worse, killed—by poor communication. For example, the vice chairman of one of the world's top investment banks told me that his company's top-rated analyst was having difficulty getting a job outside the company after having successfully completed the rigorous two-year program at the bank (it is typical that Wall Street firms help their analysts get jobs—often in private equity—following their two-year programs). In diagnosing why, his coworkers discovered that the analyst was a poor interviewer. Around the office, he was known to be brilliant, supremely hardworking, insightful, and responsive. But in interviews, he came across as forlorn in his tone and long-winded when answering questions. In this he contrasted with the company's lowest-rated analyst, who interviewed for a job in private equity and received an offer on the spot because he was so good at communicating.

If you identify more with the first analyst in the story, the good news is that interviewing is a skill that can be learned. You don't have to become a master, but the more you practice and apply Interview Tips #1 through #4, the better equipped you will be to go into interviews knowing you can represent yourself well.

To practice interviewing, you might ask a friend to give you a mock interview and record the conversation so that you can see if your body language supports or detracts from your words. (If a friend isn't available, there's always the trusty bathroom mirror.) Pay attention to your posture. Are you sitting upright? Listen to your voice and make sure you don't raise your pitch at the end of sentences, which conveys a lack of confidence. Keep a notebook to write down the phrases, words, and ideas that work and bring it to your interviews (with previously prepared questions for the particular meeting). Finally, don't feel pressured to answer every single question immediately. If you don't know the answer right away, pause. Say, "Let me think about that." Wait three seconds, collect your thoughts, and then answer.

The Telephone and Video Interview

It is common for first interviews to take place by phone or video conference. If that's the case for you, make sure that you are sitting in a quiet place with a good signal. It's difficult to create a professional impression if your call gets dropped or if there's background noise on your end of the line.

Telephone and Skype interviews will rarely secure you the job, but they are a key step in the process. Most often, the employer will use them to weed out candidates. You can expect the interviewer to set a conversational tone rather than try to intimidate, test, or trick you. Your goal, as with any step in the job search process, is to express yourself well and get to the next step, which in this case is an in-person interview.

Here's how most phone and video interviews are ordered:

The Opening

In the first minute or two, the interviewer will often bring up an icebreaker from your résumé to start the conversation in a comfortable, conversational way.

The Chronology

Next, the interviewer will say something like "Can you walk me through your résumé?" The point of this exercise is for the interviewer to begin learning who you are and how you think, as well as to understand the major influences and turning points in your life. It goes without saying that you should know your résumé well enough so that you can summon any piece of it to substantiate a point you want to make or respond to a question. You need to talk through your résumé as a story with a clear narrative arc. Make sure to work in points about your work ethic, values, and personality and find ways to weave in interesting personal details. Are you the achievement-oriented firstborn, the sensitive middle child, or the innovative third or fourth born? What character-building difficulties have you had to overcome along the way? Be very careful not to go on too long (three to five minutes is a good guideline for this). Find the right balance of telling your story and being concise. Highlight what you want to emphasize about yourself.

The Assessment

If you're interviewing for a specific job, the interviewer will next try to assess whether you meet the requirements of the position. This is the portion of the interview where preparation pays off. You should have carefully studied the posting and thought about how your experience can be tied to the requirements. Make sure to prepare one or two thoughtful points that you can recite at will. Have them written in your interview notebook.

The interviewer also might ask a question or two designed to test how you fit with their culture. Which environments have you been most effective in, and what kinds of office cultures have frustrated you? Be prepared to answer these questions earnestly and substantiate your answers with brief but specific stories.

The Conclusion

When it's time to bring the conversation to a close, the interviewer will ask you if you have any questions for them. As I stressed above, you want to have two or three insightful questions prepared. In a phone or Skype interview, you should pick one or two of your strongest questions to keep things from dragging on for too long. Make sure that the questions you ask reinforce your narrative and address topics the interviewer seemed to be concerned about. Thank the interviewer for his or her time and emphasize that you would be very interested to continue the conversation. But don't expect the interviewer to decide at this point whether there will be a next step.

Keep an eye on the clock. These interviews may last for only ten or fifteen minutes, and they rarely run more than a half hour. It's likely that you will get off the line and realize that the interviewer didn't ask you about 90 percent of what you had prepared to talk about. But fear not: this was just another step in the process. The more that you do these, the better you will get and the more effective and efficient your preparation will be.

Dress the Part

One of the trickiest parts of preparing for an interview is deciding how to dress. You don't want to be underdressed and disrespectful, but you don't want to be ridiculously overdressed and look like you don't belong. You've researched the company's culture, but it's often difficult to discern a company's norms for dress until you've already worked there.

In our research with both young professionals and business leaders, we found strong agreement that it is always better to dress on the conservative side. There are no differences between a video and an in-person interview. Look professional, but be mindful that business attire is not always appropriate for every interview situation. And, when in doubt, you can always ask the person who's setting up your interview what kind of dress is appropriate.

HOW HALEY LEARNED AN IMPORTANT LESSON ABOUT HOW TO DRESS THE PART[1]

A few weeks ago, I had the pleasure of meeting with entertainment powerhouse Nancy Armstrong, CEO of a leading television network. I met Nancy at her impeccably decorated corner office. Nancy herself is a pretty woman, with

---

[1] Name and company identity have been changed.

a triathlete's body and the kind of style you have to be successful to pull off. But besides having a glamorous wardrobe and an envy-inducing office, Nancy is a legend for having defied expectations and challenged boundaries. She worked her way up from production assistant to CEO and has turned around the fortunes of multiple TV networks along the way.

So, as you can imagine, I was nervous but also excited at the opportunity to pick her brain. The morning of our meeting, I basically tried on every article of clothing I owned, plus some from my roommates! I settled on black jeans, a white button-down shirt, a navy blazer, and my favorite loafers, which were embroidered in a camo print. It was definitely a step up from what I usually wear around the city, and I even got my hair done early on in the day. I felt I looked the best version of myself: serious and professional, but with shoes that gave me a little bit of whimsy.

My meeting with Nancy went very well. I felt like I knew the nuances of her career, and just sitting down with her brought out a very professional air in me. I was speaking in full sentences and listening before I answered! Imagine!

However, a few weeks later, Nancy had lunch with the mentor who introduced me to her. He texted me that day to call him, saying he had feedback on my meeting. My heart sank at the word "feedback." When someone tells you they have feedback, it rarely means you're going to hear something positive. But I bit my fist and called him back. And the feedback was, as expected, not positive. However, it wasn't that I was unprepared for the meeting or that I talked too much—it was that my outfit was too casual. Too casual! You mean my black jeans, white button-down shirt, navy blazer, and funky loafer combo was too low-key? Yes. It was.

The point of this story is that I'm an amazing interviewee! Just kidding. The point is that I blew my first impression, and I had no idea that's what I was doing. I could have easily dressed more formally had I known this would have been a thing. It reminded me of a podcast where Amy Schumer talks with some well-known comedians and discusses how, when she first met them, she was afraid to even speak, let alone sit at their table. She felt like she had to earn that. In the same way, I had to earn my place at Nancy's table, but my outfit made her think I was entitled. I had to earn the jeans-loafer combo, even if the jeans were black and the shoes were trendy. So, if you're under six feet tall, rock the heels-suit combo. And for someone taller, like me—well, let's just say I wholeheartedly invested in one of those power dresses that shows off your Michelle Obama biceps but has a hemline suitable for synagogue.

Make Sure to Follow Up

After your interview, don't forget to send a thank-you note. It should be thoughtful and concise, and you should send it immediately. As with many other steps, this obviously won't get you the job. But a potential employer will notice if you skip this step. If you've done in-person interviews and met multiple people on the visit, take the time to send individual notes to each person. A brief, well-written note reinforces your professionalism, and it's also a good occasion for asking about next steps.

—⊝—

The more you interview, the more you will hone your skills and come to feel as if your performance in the interviews is a strength, not a handicap. Your narrative will become sharper as you test what resonates with different interviewers, and you will know how to prepare and how to dress to create the best impression. All of this will translate into increased confidence, which will in turn make you more effective and at ease when you're in the hot seat. If you invest the time and effort in sharpening your interviewing skills, it will pay dividends throughout your career.

DECIDING WHAT JOB TO ACCEPT

"The right job will put you in a situation where you are forced to be responsible for yourself and where you are challenged intellectually, creatively, and otherwise. It has to be hard, it has to tax your imagination and effort."

—MALCOLM GLADWELL

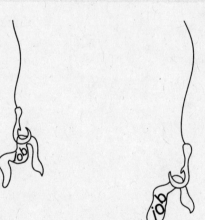

When Marissa Mayer graduated from Stanford in 1999 with a master's degree in computer science, she had a sophisticated method for deciding which of her (fourteen!) job offers to accept. She built a detailed spreadsheet of all the things she was looking for in a job, and she plotted each offer against those criteria. After an eight-hour conversation with a friend, Marissa decided to join a Web start-up, where she would be the twentieth employee and the first female engineer. As you might know, that start-up was called Google, and over the next thirteen years Marissa would go on to become one of the most successful and visible leaders in Silicon Valley, eventually becoming Yahoo!'s CEO in July 2012.

Years later, Marissa said that her decision to join Google was one of her best calls ever—but not because Google turned out to be wildly successful, or because her job there helped her to become CEO of a well-known company. She is proud of her decision because she chose Google on the basis of the opportunity to work with the smartest people she could find, people who would push her to learn and grow. That might or might not be the most important thing for you, but it was for her. By following the value most important to her, Marissa chose a job that helped her to become the success she is today.

Few people are afforded the range of opportunities that Marissa had, and even fewer will join a start-up that ends up becoming one of the most valuable companies in the world. But we can all learn from the approach she used when deciding which job to accept.[1] In

---

[1] It should be noted that Marissa, one of the most logical, intelligent executives I've ever met (much less recruited), has long been consis-

our survey of young professionals, more than half of the respondents reported that they too had had the opportunity to decide between multiple options. But even if you don't have fourteen companies knocking at your door, it's essential to consider carefully which factors are most important to you in your work life.

So let us turn to the question of how to decide which job is right for you.

The Right Job or the Right Company? That Is the Question

What is more important to you: getting into the right *job* or getting into the right *company*?

The right *job* is one that pays well, offers meaningful work, puts you under the direction of a good boss, and includes opportunities for advancement. The right *company* is one that is well known and respected, offering good training and a brand that you're proud to be associated with.

A majority of the young professionals we surveyed believe that getting into the right job, regardless of the company, is more important than getting into the right organization. But when their answers are compared to those of senior business leaders, the answer is not as clear. On the basis of our survey results, a mentor or

---

tent in her decision-making approach. As a high school senior she had been accepted to each of the ten colleges to which she applied, and she did a similar priority-weighted analysis that eventually led her to Stanford.

parent is likely to advise you that the organization is more important than the job. And more than three-quarters of the top leaders we surveyed advised that the right company or organization is most important for young professionals starting out in their careers.

If this chart were to be turned into a dialogue, it might go something like this:

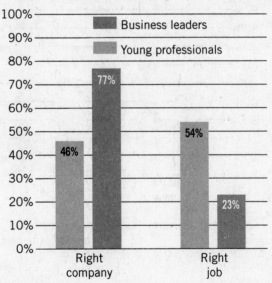

WHAT IS MORE IMPORTANT?

Starting at the right company? Or in the right job?
A comparison of young professionals and business leaders.

- Business Leader (or Parent): *Just get your foot in the door at a respected company, and opportunities will open up.*
- Young Professional: *But I want to be in a place where I can have a big impact—and I'm concerned that if I don't start in the right job, I may find myself in a dead end.*

This is a challenging dilemma, especially since it's impossible to peer ahead into the future and find out for sure whether you will enjoy a job, or whether the position will lead to something more. But there's an additional layer to our survey data that may help frame your thinking on the question.

WHAT IS MORE IMPORTANT?

Starting at the right company? Or in the right job?
A comparison of young professionals and business leaders.

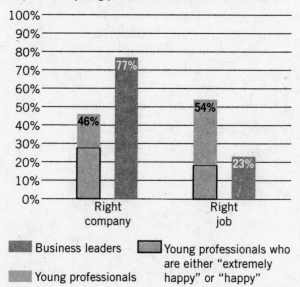

More than half of the young professionals who chose the company over the job indicated that they were "happy" or "extremely happy." By contrast, only one-third of the young professionals who said that getting the right job was most important reported that they were either happy or extremely happy. While I don't want to draw too definitive a conclusion from these numbers, they do suggest a couple of important points about happiness as it relates to your career. As detailed in chapter 4 about relationships and networks, the single most important factor leading to happiness at work is the quality of your relationships.[2] And there is a direct connection between the strength of an organization and the opportunity to build enriching relationships. The fact is that winning companies attract higher-caliber people and tend to have more positive cultures that foster the collaboration and shared experiences that in turn lead to quality relationships.

Go "Blue Chip" Early

My personal view on this question is that you should "go blue chip" early. The organizations you work for early in your career will always be part of your story. In the same way that attending Harvard, Stanford, or Oxford makes you a strong candidate for an entry-level job, joining the "best" company early in your career will give you a credibility that can open doors as your professional life unfolds.

I can't tell you how many times I've watched boards of directors evaluate the quality of a *CEO* candidate

---

[2] One hundred percent of the business leaders and 97 percent of the young professionals cited "the quality of my relationships" as one of the most important factors that led to their happiness—more than health, personal impact, and money.

on the basis of the first organization he or she worked for. For example, one search committee had this to say about a forty-five-year-old e-commerce executive who had spent her first seven years at General Electric: "Well, she had her foundational experience at GE, so she learned what it's like to operate a business and hold others accountable." Granted, it's more difficult to make connections like this today, when the "right" organization might employ only twenty or thirty people. But I still believe that joining a blue-chip organization is more likely to provide you with the opportunity to build friendships with other outstanding people, people who will go on to achieve great things and support you in your efforts to do the same.

As with most things career related, landing a first job at a blue-chip company is easier said than done. You may be offered only a minimum-wage internship or a potentially dead-end job in a prestigious company. If you find yourself in this dilemma, how should you decide whether to accept?

First, make sure to ask the hiring manager some questions:

- *Over the past three years, how many interns have you had, and how many were offered full-time roles?*
- *What is your company's track record of moving young people laterally from one group to another? How does that work in practice?*
- *What is the person who last held this job doing today?*

> • *What kinds of people are most successful in the*
> *organization? What are the common character-*
> *istics of those who don't make the grade?*

It goes without saying that you shouldn't be so overt that you come across as wanting an entirely different job than the one for which you're being considered. But you can ask about the opportunities for growth and the career tracks of others who have worked in the position.

If the company's practice and culture is to "start in the mail room" and move up from there—as is the case in talent agencies and companies like UPS, where almost everyone starts as a driver—that might give you the confidence you need to take the leap.

Alternatively, if you receive a good offer from an organization you don't quite love, you might ask yourself a different set of questions:

> • *Have people moved from this company to others*
> *that I admire?*
> • *Will the job push me to learn valuable new skills?*
> • *How will this role help me figure out if this is the*
> *right kind of job for me?*
> • *As I look around the company, do I see people*
> *who seem to share my interests and values?*

In both cases, you can look up people from that company on LinkedIn to see how *they've* moved internally or where they went afterward. This will give you real insights into whether the job—and company—are right for you.

**READER
ALERT**

SOMETIMES, PURSUING THE COMPANY AND NOT THE POSITION CAN COST YOU THE JOB

Lauren, a college senior with a passion for retail, wanted to start her career at Bloomingdale's, one of the most respected companies in the field. She had done her homework and was ready to do whatever it took to work for this blue-chip company. She went in for an interview and told the HR director that she would be happy joining either of their two training programs, one for merchandising, the other for store operations. This turned out to be a mistake.

The HR manager said that the two training programs were so different no one could possibly be interested in both. She was put off that Lauren had not come into the conversation with a sense of which program was right for her. Lauren wanted to start her career at Bloomingdale's, and she was willing to do so in either training program— but that wasn't what the interviewer wanted to hear.

The lesson here is that while getting into the right company may be a wise strategy, you still need to have a well-developed sense of what specifically you want to do at the company. Even if you don't really mind, you still need to be able to make the case not just for "Why Bloomingdale's?" but "Why this specific job?"

Other Factors to Consider

Beyond the right job/right company debate, which other factors should you consider when sorting through your options? There are, of course, the three dimensions of the Career Triangle: job quality, lifestyle, and pay. But at a more detailed level, what other attributes should you consider?

In our survey results, there are areas of overlap and notable differences between what business leaders and people in the early stages of their careers believe. Business leaders said almost unanimously that company culture and fit should be your top priority in choosing a job. Young professionals agree that culture is important, but they don't rank it quite as high. Business leaders advise young professionals to consider the organization's CEO and top management team; after all, the company's culture starts at the top. As discussed in chapter 3 about money, business leaders and young professionals value compensation differently. Another disparity has to do with the preferred size of the organization. Business leaders prefer the greater resources that large companies offer, while young professionals often prefer smaller companies with more entrepreneurial environments.

While size and compensation are important, top business leaders and young professionals agree that these should take a back seat to other factors. Most important are the potential for advancement, the functional area you will be working in, and starting out in an industry that is growing or that tends to pay well.

FACTORS TO CONSIDER

When an aspiring young professional is deciding about choosing a job, to what extent should the following factors play a role?

A comparison of young professionals and business leaders

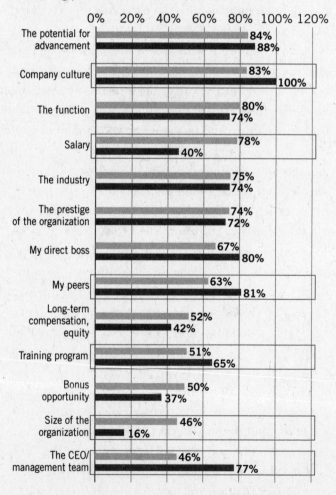

The Single Biggest Contributor to Job Satisfaction

Over the last twenty years, Gallup has conducted millions of workplace surveys, covering just about every aspect of professional life. One of their most important and actionable findings is that employees' job satisfaction is the single biggest determinant of how effective they will be in their role. It is also one of the most important contributors to their happiness outside of work.

But here's where the findings are surprising. According to Gallup's research, job satisfaction can be boiled down to one single question:

> *Do you have someone you consider a best friend at work?*

If you can answer "yes" to this question, chances are you are happy with your job—the reason being that the conditions for forming genuine friendships are the same conditions that make people enjoy working for an organization: an office environment of trust and support, coworkers who are pleasing to be around, a workplace where you can feel at home, and the opportunity to form relationships there that nourish you.

So when it comes to deciding what job to accept, here are three questions that you might ask:

- *Do I like and respect the people I would be working with on a daily basis?*
- *Is the environment and culture one in which I can truly be myself?*

- *Are the most senior leaders people I would like to emulate?*

If you can answer yes to these questions, you might just be looking at the company that's right for you. And who knows, maybe it will even become the next Google.

Part 3

HOW TO *THRIVE*

10

GETTING OFF TO THE RIGHT START IN A NEW JOB

When you start off in a new job, you get only one chance to make a first impression. And, as you know from experience, *first impressions can become lasting ones*. First impressions are important because they often set the tone for how people in your organization will come to view and treat you for as long as you work there. Are you the person everyone is excited to work with? Or are there "concerns" about whether you're going to make it at the company? By the end of your first few weeks, many of your coworkers will have privately assigned you to one of these two categories.

Larry Summers, former president of Harvard University, came up with a mathematical metaphor for describing how your reputation is built in your first few weeks on the job. "People form their impressions as an average," he says. "If they've had only two impressions of you and they get a third, then it could move you as much as three halves. But if they've had ninety-six impressions so far and they get a ninety-seventh, it won't have a big impact."

If this worries you, the good news is that the first impressions you make in a new job are mostly under your control. Why? Because they depend less on your performance and more on your attitude and conduct at the office.

Many of the strategies for getting off to the right start in a job are so straightforward they almost don't bear writing about. But it's worth spending the next couple of pages on how to make sure your first impressions are good ones. The headlines are that you should have a positive attitude, be polite to *everyone* you interact with, communicate effectively, conduct yourself like a professional, work hard, ask lots of questions, and do a killer job on every task you take on. Let's look at each of these strategies, and a handful of others, in more detail.

Nothing Is More Important Than a Positive Attitude

Your attitude is the one thing over which you have complete control, and it turns out to be critical to your success in any new job. Be positive and enthusiastic. Create energy in meetings and off-the-cuff conversations; don't be a downer. Jump on any chance you get to learn a new skill or process, and maintain an abundance mentality, where the more you can help others, the better it is for you. Never say, "That's not my job." Always be willing to help out.

When you're adapting to a new job or work environment, you might be under a lot of pressure as you try to find your bearings. But believe it or not, the senior people in your organization probably envy you. Seriously. Even the most successful of executives are nostalgic for the days when they were young, when the future was ahead of them and they had the energy to work hard and play hard. So take advantage of that nostalgia by having fun in your job, building strong relationships, and conducting yourself in a way that makes your colleagues and supervisors enjoy being around you.

Be Effective in *All* Your Communications

To create a strong impression in your early days on the job—and, frankly, throughout your career—it is essential to be effective in all your communications.

When you speak, whether in meetings or casual conversations, pay attention to the tone and clarity of your voice. Enunciate your words and remember to project. Avoid using verbal crutches and fillers—such as *um, like, you know,* and *I mean*—and make sure you don't raise the pitch of your voice at the end of sentences. Verbal tics like these can make you sound less confident, or worse, unintelligent.

One form of communication that often gets overlooked is *nonverbal* communication. The way you look and carry yourself has a disproportionate influence on how others perceive you, especially in your early days on the job. Experts have found that the way you carry yourself influences people's impressions of you even more than the actual words you speak. Taken together, your verbal and nonverbal communications translate directly into your executive presence: the way in which your coworkers and superiors perceive you. Are you a serious player who, despite being new on the job, can be sought out for opinions? Or are you a lightweight who doesn't have anything of substance to say? The more substantial your executive presence, the more successful you will be in your career. So maintain eye contact when speaking to others, and always make sure to have a firm handshake. Be conscious of your posture and the facial expressions you project to others. Even if you don't intend to keep others at bay, a cold or uninterested expression can discourage them from engaging with you.

When starting a new job, it's critical that you learn how to present well. Meetings and formal presentations are often the stage on which you make or break your reputation. So make sure that you know how to communicate effectively when speaking in front of a group. Practice often, take lessons on the side if necessary, and seek out feedback that will help you increase your confidence. Try out different presentation techniques and find the style that works for you. If you can, try to work a well-timed sense of humor into your presentations, as it will set people at ease and keep them engaged.

Read the news. Stay informed on what's happening

in the world, and weave current events and news from your industry into your presentations and daily interactions. Share interesting articles, posts, and news with your colleagues when you think it might interest them or add value to something you're working on together.

One of the pitfalls to avoid in your early days—and really, at any time in your career—is conducting yourself in a way that makes people think you're a know-it-all. Nobody likes working with people who think they're always right, and the fact is, know-it-alls usually know a lot less than they think.

When you are starting in a new position, you won't have all the answers, nor should you expect to. But what you *should* have is an open mind and a curious disposition. Ask lots of questions, and be a receiver of information, not a broadcaster. In this way, you will keep yourself open to new perspectives and increase your chances of generating valuable new insights and discoveries.

E-Mail Etiquette

As I mentioned in Part 2, e-mail has become an important tool for convenient professional communication, but it's easy to use in a way that can make you come across as unprofessional. So in your first weeks on the job, take care to establish good habits for managing your e-mail correspondence. Find a system for keeping your inbox organized and responding quickly to colleagues' e-mails—whether it means using folders, color coding, or alerts. You may even need to spend time in the evenings or on the weekend cleaning out your inbox and responding to important messages.

Remember: Work e-mails are serious business. They are not texts or tweets, and you can get fired for sending e-mails with off-color jokes or insensitive comments. E-mails are permanently discoverable, and most corporate IT departments monitor their employees' messages. You don't want to be too stiff or impersonal, but do your best to keep your e-mails professional, and err on the side of formality—especially in your early days on the job.

Take the time to craft well-written e-mails, as your written communication will speak volumes about your intelligence and professionalism. Use good grammar, double-check for typos, and always do your best to be concise. The easier your messages are to read, the better. Don't use fonts smaller than 11 points. It's likely that your e-mail will be read on a handheld device, or by a senior colleague whose eyesight will be strained by small lettering.

Make Yourself Visible

In your early days on the job, make yourself visible to your colleagues and supervisors. Be one of the first people to arrive every morning and one of the last to leave. Don't miss work or ask if you can work remotely, at least for your first few months.

Take time to walk around the office and talk to people. Introduce yourself—not once, not twice, but as many times as it takes for people to actually remember your name. Most people aren't good at remembering names, so don't assume someone will remember yours after one introduction. That being said, people will be flattered if you commit *their* name to memory. One way to do this is to repeat their name immediately after you're introduced. You could even keep a notebook where you take down notes about each new person you meet. If you keep a notebook of your early interactions, you'll be surprised at how valuable it can become as you move into later months and years in your job. You will be able to go back and pull out facts about people and details from earlier conversations that will link one meeting to another, and in the process you'll differentiate yourself from the people for whom every interaction seems to start from scratch.

Ask lots of questions about the work of your colleagues and acquaintances. How long have they worked for the organization, and how did they get there? If someone is known for having an open door, drop by every once in a while. Ask if you can listen in on a conference call. If appropriate, ask them to get a coffee with you, go to breakfast or lunch, or grab a beer after hours. All of this will show that you care about the people you meet and are interested in learning about how all parts of the organization work.

Being visible also means dressing the part. You want to look sharp and fit into the norms of the organization—but during your first weeks and months on a job, you might try dressing 20 percent more formally than is the norm, which will create an air of professionalism. This may require you to spend money on new clothes, but it's worth it. Your dress says a lot about your level of professionalism and self-respect.

Speaking of professionalism, pay attention to how you act outside the office. Now that you're employed, you are representing the brand of your organization, whether or not you happen to be sitting at your desk. Be careful about what you post (or are tagged in) on social media, and make sure all of your online profiles put forth an appropriate and positive impression.

Finally, be polite to *everyone* you interact with—especially your office's executive assistants and receptionists. They are the nervous system of your organization, and their impression of you will almost certainly influence your rapport with the company's senior leaders. They also hold troves of knowledge about the way things get done around the office. Cultivate relationships with them. If you send their boss an e-mail, make sure to copy them, and never go around them when scheduling meetings with their boss. Just as senior professionals never like to be surprised with news, an executive assistant never wants to be outside his or her boss's flow of information.

Study and Soak Up Your Company's Culture

In every organization there are unwritten protocols, unspoken taboos, and hidden networks through which important information gets spread. In your job interview, you might have been given an official description of how the organization works, but once you're employed by the company it's time to begin paying at-

tention to how things *really* work around there. Solicit
the advice of coworkers when you're trying to find your
bearings at the company—but, at the end of the day,
the onus is on you to figure out the norms that define
your organization's culture and accepted behavior.

To this end, the first thing you should do is revisit
all of the preparation you did when you first started
researching the company. Review the notes you took in
your interviews, as well as the articles and social media
postings you were able to find. Then, when you get the
chance to speak with long-standing employees in your
first few weeks on the job, ask some more specific questions, like:

- *What do the people who are most successful have
  in common?*
- *Who are the most respected people in the organization? Why?*
- *What are the commonalities among those who
  haven't worked out?*

You can also learn a lot by taking note of the specific words your supervisors and colleagues frequently
use. Every company has a set of words, acronyms,
phrases, or professional jargon that gets picked up by
its employees, and these words say a lot about what the
company values. At Boston Consulting Group, employees talk about problem solving and thought leadership.
At NBC Universal, people talk about ratings and OCF
(operating cash flow). At Capital One, employees talk
about how the best modeling and data analytics enable
them to offer financial services to people who wouldn't
otherwise have access. At Bridgewater, the culture is

described by "radical transparency," and at Cisco Systems, it's all about customer wins. What words do you notice people using at your office?

Put on your anthropologist hat, and go sleuthing for cultural clues. Pay attention to how people interact with one another in the hallways and cafeteria. Do they look happy or stressed out? Do the architecture, furniture, and artwork in the office create an informal and upbeat physical environment? Do people's offices have lots of light and open spaces that encourage easy interaction among employees, or do they have walled hallways and closed doors that convey a more rigid culture?

LEARN TO TALK ABOUT SPORTS, CULTURE, AND OTHER AREAS OF MUTUAL INTEREST

You've probably heard of Mike Krzyzewski, the renowned head coach of Duke University's basketball team and the winningest men's coach in college basketball history. But you probably haven't heard of Sanyin Siang, an expert on leadership, ethics, and technology who has partnered with Coach K to bring his leadership formula from the basketball court to the world of business. Sanyin offers a helpful piece of tactical advice for those looking to make good impressions and accelerate developing relationships at the office:

Become comfortable talking about areas of mutual interest, such as sports, pop culture, fashion, art, and music.

"One of the keys to relationship building," Sanyin says, "is communicating with one's audience in a language that

resonates with them." And, to that end, Sanyin has de-
tected an unmistakable pattern among the CEOs she advises: "They tend to have great sports awareness."

It may sound frivolous, but it's remarkable how often
areas of interest like sports, television shows, and movies
come up in conference rooms before a presentation starts,
during pleasantries at the beginning of a client meeting, or
even at the outset of a job interview. If you become liter-
ate in sports and other "extracurricular" topics, it can pay
dividends in these kinds of settings, where informal but
important judgments are made.

Form an Effective Relationship with Your Boss

Another key to success in a new job is establishing a
productive relationship with your manager. There's no
single person who has more direct influence on your
first couple of years than your boss, and the habits and
rapport you establish with him or her will become a
crucial factor in your short- and medium-term success.

Intelligent bosses instinctively separate the people
they manage into three distinct categories: the syco-
phants, the contrarians, and the small percentage of
employees who are balanced players. You want your
boss to see you as the third kind of person.

Work to understand your boss's motivations. Most
managers will say their most important goals are to
grow the business, drive revenue, control costs, develop
a winning strategy, make sound investments, and
manage people effectively. While these ambitions are
usually genuine, most managers have unstated motives

about their own success that turn out to be just as important.

According to David D'Alessandro, former CEO of insurance giant John Hancock Financial Services and author of the bestseller *Career Warfare*, "What bosses want more than anything else is loyalty, good advice, and to have 'their personal brands polished.'" With this in mind, take care to never make yourself look good at the boss's expense. If you circumvent your supervisor, you will be seen as breaking the chain of command, and it will reflect poorly on you, even if you happen to be right about the issue at hand.

As you begin to develop working rhythms in your new job, solicit feedback on how your boss thinks you're performing. Don't wait for formal review cycles—use important projects or even occasional downtime at the office as opportunities to ask for feedback.

High-Quality Work Is Your Ticket to Play . . . Even on Menial Tasks

Many young professionals enter the workforce ready to save the world, only to quickly become disillusioned when they find themselves sitting in a cubicle in front of a computer screen. Such is often the plight in an entry-level job, where your actual day-to-day work may not fully engage your potential or match up with your long-term picture of success. But even in the most menial of roles, it's worth remembering that distinctive performance is and will always be your ticket to play—

the experience that enables you to move on to something more exciting and rewarding.

Everyone has to start somewhere, and for most people, "somewhere" is the bottom. Though you may not be able to necessarily see the tangible impact of your daily work, it doesn't diminish the fact that you are building valuable skills that will aid you in your early days and throughout the course of your career.

So consider what is being asked of you and why, and then deliver. Make sure your numbers and reports make sense. Spend extra time ensuring that your PowerPoint presentations tell a coherent story, supported with well-designed charts and graphs. Proofread your written communication. Look for hidden points in your analysis that can raise thought-provoking questions, hypotheses, or observations. Be prepared to say something interesting when someone asks, "What do you think?" Put yourself in the shoes of whoever it is that will be reviewing your work, and think about how you can make *their* life easier. Hold your work to the standard that, should your boss share it with his or her bosses and colleagues, they too will come away impressed. The key is to do all of your tasks—even the seemingly unimportant ones—in an exceptional way. This will differentiate you from many others.

⊖

Your career is a marathon, not a sprint. No matter how ambitious and adept you are, it's important to set realistic expectations at the outset for the kind of work you will be doing and how long it will take you to advance. But a marathon has to start somewhere, and if you start by establishing the office habits from this chapter, it will enable you to get off to the right start in your new job and create real momentum that will set you up for success over the long term.

FOUR GUARANTEED STRATEGIES FOR SUCCESS

This chapter aims to build on the momentum you will have achieved by the time you've figured out your strategy within the framework of how careers really work. It aims to extend your hard work of finding a job and getting off to a strong start. You may already be in an organization or well into your career, and, if so, I hope some of the key lessons that we've reviewed thus far—such as the power of relationships and networks, how to operate like a professional, and how to tell a narrative and communicate effectively—will continue to power your success. There are at least four strategies that, when coupled with all of this, will support your success throughout your career.

Success Strategy #1: Focus on the Success of Others

I had the opportunity to ask Richard Branson, billionaire founder of Virgin Atlantic Airways, what advice he would offer to aspiring young professionals.[1]

---

[1] Sir Richard Branson is one of the most iconic entrepreneurs in the world. Over the last forty-seven years he has built a global empire,

"This may sound simplistic," he said, "but always look for the best in others. Be compassionate and praise the people you work with." Those who conduct themselves like this, he said, "will get on with others and, by extension, get the best results." When Branson spots a Virgin employee who isn't a decent person or doesn't treat others kindly, he does his best to move him or her out of the organization immediately.

If you carry away one piece of advice from this chapter, I hope it will be this:

> Success is achieved by making those around you successful.

It is also as close to a guaranteed success strategy as can exist in today's environment.

Right now, it may not seem that focusing on the success of others is more important than your individual performance. Indeed, as I noted earlier, your performance and the quality of your work really do matter—especially when you're trying to get off to the right start in a new job. But that doesn't mean the

---

with interests ranging from Virgin Atlantic Airways, Virgin Mobile, Virgin Money, and Virgin Trains, to charitable enterprise Virgin Unite and the space tourism enterprise Virgin Galactic, not to mention his private Caribbean getaway, Necker Island. For many around the world, he is the very embodiment of success, having achieved fame and fortune, massive commercial success, a globally renowned brand, a reputation for fun and adventure, and prolific followership (he has 6.7 million followers on LinkedIn and has published over ten bestselling books). Self-described as a "tie-loathing adventurer and thrill seeker, who believes in turning ideas into reality," Richard left school at age 16, and his first venture was the creation of *Student Magazine*. That was the initial step in what has become Virgin Group, which today comprises some 360 companies.

workplace needs to be a treacherous place, in which the higher you climb in your career the more cutthroat you must become.

Contrary to what you may believe, most highly successful business leaders are not overly self-centered people. In my research and professional experience, the most successful top executives spend as much time thinking about the success of their company and their direct reports as they spend thinking about their own success. Here's a snapshot from one part of our research. We asked young professionals and top business leaders: *Do you spend more time and energy thinking about your own success or about the success of those around you?* Here's how they answered:

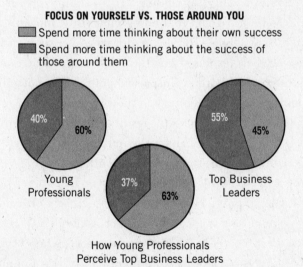

FOCUS ON YOURSELF VS. THOSE AROUND YOU
▨ Spend more time thinking about their own success
▨ Spend more time thinking about the success of those around them

40% / 60%

Young Professionals

37% / 63%

How Young Professionals Perceive Top Business Leaders

55% / 45%

Top Business Leaders

The majority of young professionals self-report that they spend more time and energy thinking about their own success. At the same time, they estimate that top business leaders care about their own success to an even greater degree. But in our survey, top leaders self-report that they care more about the success of those around them than their own success—and further research backs up the top executives' answers.

For my book *The Five Patterns of Extraordinary Careers,* we asked over two thousand senior managers to describe the most successful person they knew. Nearly 90 percent said that the most successful person cared about the careers of his or her subordinates as much as—or even more than—his or her own career. Further, only 4 percent of top executives were described by their peers and subordinates as being concerned first with their own careers.

Some are highly confident take-charge taskmasters, some are charismatic and charming, and others are humble and self-effacing. But whatever their style, the very best leaders share the ability to create an environment of trust and transparency, of commitment and energy, where each employee knows how his or her role fits into the organization's results and how collective success will in turn benefit the individual.

Guhan Selvaretnam, most recently the senior vice president of the TV Networks Group in Discovery Digital Media, provides a memorable, if slightly off-color, analogy of how to focus on the success of others. "How you treat people matters, regardless of where they sit," he says. "The corporate hierarchy is like a bunch of monkeys sitting on a tree. The monkeys on the top branches look at the monkeys below and all they see looking up at them are smiling faces. However, the monkeys below look at the monkeys above, and all they see staring down at them are assholes. Don't be a monkey, and try to avoid working for a monkey. The only thing you own in your career is how you treat everyone, regardless of where they sit on that tree!"

People crave leadership and direction. They enjoy working for companies with bold, clearly defined aspirations, and organizations where team behavior is governed by a strong sense of ethics and shared values. Most important, when a team's members are focused on one another's success, creativity reigns because people feel free to be honest and question authority without retribution. Each member of the team feels just as accountable to the others as to the leader, and the work environment is marked by loyalty and exceptional strong performance.

In the early stages of your career, you won't have the power to set your company's culture from the top down. But there are still ways that you can focus on the success of others. You can help create a trustful working environment by making sure communications flow freely and by pitching in when colleagues need help.

The concept of making those around you successful is effective not only in business but in other aspects of life as well. Jim Quigley, retired chairman and CEO of Deloitte, calls it "the Battier Effect," the ability to help others succeed. He coined this term with reference to Shane Battier, one of the best team players ever to play basketball. In his final two seasons with the NBA champion Miami Heat, Shane led the league in one statistic: time of possession. Not the longest time of possession but *the shortest*. The average time that Shane possessed the basketball every time he got it was ... *one second*.

"For all the hours I spent practicing, dribbling, shooting, and passing," Shane told me, "I only possessed the ball 2 percent of my time on the court." The other 98 percent was spent playing smothering defense, setting picks, moving the ball to open teammates, and coaching and encouraging his teammates. This is what led Shane to be voted NBA Teammate of the Year in his final season in 2014. "How was it that I could succeed in the NBA, when I was told I was too slow, too nice, and couldn't jump?" he asks. "It was that I was totally focused on making my teammates successful."

BEING A LEADER ON AND OFF THE FIELD

In college I played goalkeeper for the women's soccer team, but at the beginning of my senior year I found out that the school had recruited a new keeper from the Boston area. She was *really* good. In preseason scrimmages we competed for the starting job, but when the season started, the coach chose the other keeper to start over me.

I was crushed. I had been starting ever since my freshman year. I had never *not* been the best, and a lot of thoughts were running through my mind: Should I blame the coach, try to sabotage the new goalie, quit? I was embarrassed, and I felt like a failure.

Around that time, I remembered having read about the philosophy of focusing on the success of others and I felt inspired. It was a real turning point. I swallowed my pride, embraced my role as second string, and committed to do anything I could to help the new goalkeeper succeed. I would sprint over during halftime to greet her and recap the half, and I brought her water when she was in goal. I

> hardly got any playing time that year, but it didn't mat-
> ter—I truly felt happy and successful. I also learned how
> to be part of a team. After the season, our coach called me
> in and told me what an honor it was for her to see me grow
> as a player and a person.
>
> **—CLARE, TWENTY-FIVE**

Success Strategy #2: Don't Quit (and Other Lessons from Navy SEALs)

People tend to think their successes rest on merit while their setbacks can be explained by bad luck. It's human nature. But a lot of your success will be based on something you do control—hard work and perseverance.

Admiral Eric T. Olson is a distinguished former U.S. military officer who now works in the private sector as a professor at Columbia University and as a board member for Under Armour and Iridium Communications. After a career as a U.S. Navy SEAL, he was the first naval officer ever to be appointed as commander of U.S. Special Operations Command (SOCOM), where he directed the most elite units of the U.S. military, including the Army Rangers and Special Forces, the Navy SEALs, and their special operations counterparts in the U.S. Air Force and U.S. Marine Corps.[2]

The skills Eric learned in his Navy SEAL training have served him well in his encore career, and they contain an insight that will serve you well in yours:

---

[2] SEAL is an acronym for "SEa-Air-Land."

> If you want to make it through Navy SEAL
> training—or anything else in life—don't quit.

Of the one thousand recruits who enter the rigorous six-month-long SEAL training course each year, only 200 to 250 complete it. When Eric was in charge of SEAL training, he wanted to understand what separated the successes from those who didn't make it. He found that the successful SEAL candidates were driven and focused, and were excellent problem solvers who knew how to analyze challenges from different angles under duress. But Eric didn't think these qualities explained the difference in outcomes, so he consulted a study the navy had previously run on the subject.

The study found that for the recruits who didn't make it to the end of SEAL training, the reason was not that they didn't have the skills to perform well enough. As it turned out, those who failed to complete the program did so because they *decided* to drop out.

And this decision rarely was made in the middle of a demanding exercise, or when recruits were out in the field, braving the cold, wet, or otherwise inhospitable conditions. Most candidates quit over breakfast or lunch, at a time when they were *anticipating* how difficult the day ahead would be. They chose to eliminate themselves from the program not because they were failing to perform the necessary tasks but because they feared that the coming challenges would be too difficult.

When analyzing the recruits who did complete the training, the study found that candidates who had a background in competitive water polo or wrestling had the best chance of completing the program. But they also learned that chess players were three times more likely to succeed than the average candidate.

"Chess players are always thinking two or three moves ahead," Eric explains. "They are less concerned with the current predicament. They are less emotional, less knee-jerky, and are always thinking about longer-term problem solving. Put another way, chess players don't quit over breakfast or lunch."

"I know it sounds flippant," he says, "but the key message to SEAL candidates is, don't quit. Don't quit in anticipation of future failure. Decide now to not quit, decide to keep going with the confidence that you can do more than you think you can do, despite the pain, cold, heat, sand, and fatigue that you will inevitably face."

Even if you don't have ambitions of becoming a SEAL, the message is clear. You have the power to make it through challenging, stressful times—you just need to decide that you can. Or, as Henry Ford put it, "Whether you think you can or think you can't, you're right."

> "A good career means work. And work means getting up every day and actually practicing your craft. It's not rocket science."
>
> **—HALEY, TWENTY-FOUR**

Success Strategy #3: Play to Your Strengths

Another prerequisite, both for job performance and for fulfillment in life, is to work in a role that you're good at. As I wrote when describing the six phases of your career, one of the key objectives of the Promise Phase is to navigate yourself into a job where your natural skills and talents are highly useful and valued.

We all have an intuitive sense of our strengths and weaknesses. But one way to diagnose what you're really good at is to build a skills and accomplishments inventory. Start with a blank sheet and make a chronological list of your most significant accomplishments and experiences, across your most important academic courses and extracurricular projects, internships, and jobs. Then, next to each accomplishment, note the things about the role that you enjoyed most, liked least, and performed in especially well. Then for each experience, assess the key skills and attributes that were required. Be thoughtful and try to get beyond the obvious. Are you strong-willed, self-sufficient, pragmatic, spontaneous, fun-loving, altruistic, tolerant, relational, sensitive, rule-abiding, predictable, detached, or forgiving; a competitor, an explorer, a healer, a survivor?

After filling up a few screens or sheets of paper, you will notice themes emerging. Specific strengths and weaknesses are likely to show repeatedly across the different things you've accomplished. These attributes will tend to stick with you over the course of your career. Are you short-tempered with people but patient with projects? Are you a good motivator but poor at delegation? Are you a good presenter, or do you panic in front of a crowd? Are you led by facts and analysis, or do you lean toward generating ideas and concepts? Do you thrive in the thrill of the hunt, or are you more comfortable designing products or programs? Do you love the action of financial markets, or do you feel trapped when reckoning with events outside your control? Are you on board with working on Black Friday, New Year's Eve, or other holidays, or would you prefer to leave retail and hospitality jobs to others?[3]

Whatever your perspective, and whether or not you're inspired by motivational proclamations, I believe that these exercises in self-assessment and self-discovery will help you strategically as you manage your career. They will also be invaluable when it comes to interviewing for jobs and responding persuasively to questions about your interests, strengths, and weaknesses.

Success Strategy #4: Be a "Learning Animal"

Another guaranteed success strategy is to become a *learning animal*: someone who is curious about the world around him or her, has the confidence to ask

---

[3] There are also many other resources to help you diagnose your strengths and weaknesses. The one I personally have had the most positive experience with is a self-assessment program run by the Johnson O'Connor Research Foundation, a nonprofit scientific and educational organization that has been measuring people's aptitudes and their effect on performance, success, and professional satisfaction since 1922. The foundation offers personalized programs that create individualized inventories of your aptitudes and then draw implications for careers.

questions, and works hard to understand things more deeply.

> Have an attitude of youthful—even childlike—
> curiosity about the world around you. Have the
> self-confidence to ask questions, not to show
> how smart you are, but genuinely to under-
> stand things more deeply.

Don't just ask first-level questions. Follow up on the answers you get. Probe the whys and hows, and try to go two or three levels deeper. Talk to people who have different perspectives than you do. Practice active listening and project an openness to new information—even if it's bad news. This is a particularly important quality to have when you reach a senior level in your organization, but it also becomes more difficult at that point, because people are more inclined to tell you what they think you want to hear.

Learning agility isn't a particularly new idea, but it's an idea whose time has come. When we analyzed the hundreds of CEO searches Spencer Stuart has conducted over the years, we found that learning agility was mentioned by companies a grand total of *zero* times in searches ten years ago. In the past year, however, it has been an important factor in a great majority of CEO searches we've helped conduct.

So what makes someone a "learning animal?" According to an article in the journal *Human Resource Management*, people who have learning agility are those who:

- Seek out experiences from which to learn; are attracted to "newness".

- Enjoy delving into complex problems associated with new experiences and analyzing them by drawing contrasts and parallels and searching for meaning.
- Acquire more value from these new experiences because they have a desire to make sense out of them.
- Are skilled at simplifying and synthesizing information and at presenting their views to others.
- Perform better because they are able to apply new skills and insights to their challenges and responsibilities and bring others along for the ride.

To become a learning animal, keep these tips in mind as you consider how to manage your career:

- Be eager to learn about yourself, others, and the world around you.
- Ask questions, ask more questions . . . repeat.
- Show a fundamental interest in learning from feedback and changing your behavior as a result.
- Encourage yourself and others to experiment, think critically, and learn.

"I always thought about how much I didn't know about the markets and had unrealistic expectations of how much I really needed to master. Later I realized my bosses were winging meetings all the time and still learning every day. Now I realize that tenacity and the ability to ask the right questions can help bridge gaps in content knowledge."

—DAVID, TWENTY-NINE

─⊖─

Focus on the success of your peers, play to your strengths, become a "learning animal," and don't quit. If you make a habit of these four practices, you will reap the rewards of being a member of excellent teams, and you will become known for performing well alongside others, not in spite of them, over the long term. In time, you will attract a virtual army of people willing to fight for you and your success.

12

YOU'RE A KNIGHT, NOT A BISHOP (OR, HOW TO MOVE FROM JOB TO JOB)

The notion that careers progress upward in a straight line, with people getting promoted steadily into positions of increasing responsibility, is a false picture of how things usually work. And the notion is counterproductive as well. In your career, you often will need to move laterally in order to move forward, and sometimes you will need to make a decision that causes you to feel like you're moving in reverse.

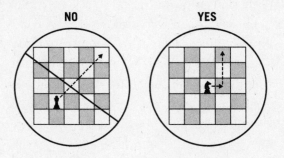

In other words, if your career were a game of chess, you would be a knight, not a bishop.

The straight, predictable path of the bishop is appealing, but your career is more likely to follow the zigzag path of the knight. The goal of this chapter is to explore how you can move from job to job—whether within your company or between organizations—and follow the knight's path to success in your career.

From the Art World to the Restaurant World—and Back Again: Hannah's Story

Hannah was an art history major at Skidmore College who dreamed of entering the art world after graduation—either at a fine arts gallery or a museum. But when Hannah won an internship at the prestigious Guggenheim Museum in New York, her dreams were thrown into question. In the internship, most of the people Hannah interacted with were pretentious, self-important, and generally unpleasant to be around. If this was what the art world was like, Hannah thought, she didn't want any part of it.

When she graduated college, Hannah moved to Italy for the summer, where she worked at Eataly, the now-famous fine food chain. At Eataly, Hannah discovered that she enjoyed working in the food industry, so when she returned to New York she focused on interviewing for restaurant positions, eventually landing a job as a coordinator for Roberta's, a hip restaurant in Brooklyn. She loved the atmosphere and the people, but after two years of working there, she realized that there was limited potential for growth within the company.

This is when Hannah decided to make a risky move. She left the relative comfort of working for a trendy restaurant, where she fit in well and was having fun, and took an entry-level job in the motion graphics industry. Hannah realized that what she loved most about the restaurant business was that it allowed her to work with a diverse group of creative people on a daily basis, and she thought she could find the same things in her new job. She started as an administrative assistant—a "backwards" move—but within her first year she was promoted to project manager. Now, six years out of college, Hannah has taken a roundabout path to doing exactly what she originally hoped to do in the fine arts world: manage creative people and help them to develop exciting new work.

This story is but one example of how a step "backwards" can leave you far ahead of where you would have been if you had tried to follow a straight line of progress in your career. Hannah started out with an idea of what she wanted to do, based on her education and interests. She tested that theory with an internship, and it helped her avoid the potential disaster of working in an industry that she didn't enjoy. So she landed a first job in a new sector that enabled her to move up a couple of levels, and when she reached a ceiling in that field she reflected honestly on her strengths and weaknesses in a way that helped her choose the career she loves today.

It Applies to CEOs Too

Consider the case of Tom, a chief executive in the entertainment industry. Tom had entered the film industry thirty years earlier, after starting his career as an English teacher. Over time, he built up a well-deserved reputation for being tough and creative and for green-lighting movies that attracted some of the largest audiences in history. Tom came to me because he had reached a crossroads in his career and wanted to apply his experience and expertise to a new job situation. In talking through his options, we decided that he could make five potential moves:

1. **Lateral Move.** He could become the CEO of a different entertainment company. The problem was, there were only a small handful of these, and at the time there weren't any openings at this high a level. But if a CEO position were to open up, Tom would certainly be one of the first people to get a call.

2. **Adjacent Move.** He could look to become CEO of a company in a different content-producing industry, such as cable television, radio, digital media, or publishing.

3. **Launch a Start-Up.** He could take his financial resources, relationships, credibility, and know-how and found an independent production company or an online content provider. He could also pursue a CEO role at a venture-backed digital media company.

4. **Move to a New Sector.** He could go a different direction and pursue his passion for and early experience in education, which might require more effort, patience, and persistence and would almost certainly be a step backwards, since it would be in an industry for which he wouldn't have executive-level experience. He could become dean of a film

or journalism school, where he could draw
on his professional expertise, or he could become head of an independent school, where
his teaching background, organizational
leadership, and ability to raise money would
be valued.

5. **Portfolio of Activities.** Finally, he could pursue multiple routes, including serving on
one or two boards, writing articles or books,
speaking, teaching, consulting, and partnering with a venture or private equity firm.

You might not have quite as many options as Tom
had (in the end he pursued opportunities in a new sector but ended up accepting a position at a new film
studio—a combination of lateral and start-up). But if
you're looking to plot your next career move, you might
try thinking through what each of these five directions
would mean for your career.

Build Skills Outside Work Before You *Have to* Make a Change

It's never too early to start building experience, skills,
and relationships outside your current organization or
sector. Life doesn't unfold along a linear path, and you
never know when you'll hit a ceiling in your current
job or suddenly feel inspired to try something new. Volunteer for not-for-profit organizations whose work interests you, and push yourself to develop rich hobbies
outside your job. Always be on the hunt for new indus-

tries and problems where your experience and perspective might be valued.

Here are some telltale signs that it's time to make a change:

- The growth rate of your compensation flattens or moves in reverse.
- The patterns in your formal feedback and reviews indicate that you aren't performing up to your expectations or the expectations the organization has for you.
- You don't feel as if people respect you as much as they did in the past.
- You're not getting access to interesting assignments or projects that you would like, and you aren't getting rewarded with growth in the scope of your responsibilities.
- Your relationship with your boss is souring, or you're coming to realize that your work environment is a toxic one.

If these signs present themselves at your current job, don't worry—everyone experiences them at one point or another; you're not alone. But if you're thinking about leaving your job, come to that conclusion thoughtfully and over time, instead of letting it dawn on you suddenly and dramatically. Talk to friends, advisers, and mentors about your frustrations and the signs that are leading you to want to make a change. Seek out their advice *before you make the decision*, instead of looking to them to affirm a decision you've already made.

If you do decide to change jobs, two moves are relatively easy to make:

1. To the same role in a different organization.
2. To a different role within the same organization.

That said, it's relatively difficult to go from one organization to another in a role that's fundamentally different or more senior than the one you're currently in. Employers feel safer hiring someone who has "been there, done that." So if you want to move to a different role or function, it's much easier to do so within your existing organization, where you ideally will have developed relationships and earned the trust of others.

Keep in mind that you don't want to make so many moves that potential employers will see you as a "job-hopper," someone who changes companies or organizations every two or three years. At the other extreme, you also don't want to be seen as a "lifer." If you're twenty years into your career and still work at the organization you joined fresh out of school, potential employers might worry that you won't be able to adapt to a new environment and succeed there.

Taking Lateral Steps All the Way to a Senior Role

Here's another reason to be a knight and not a bishop. Most companies, when looking to fill executive roles, will seek out candidates with a breadth of skills and expertise. So if your long-term goals include working in a top job, consider making lateral moves into different functional areas, new industries, and different geographical locations.

Lateral moves need to be made thoughtfully, and when done well they can demonstrate your open-mindedness, curiosity, and potential for growth. But if your career progression doesn't make sense—or if you can't explain it in a coherent narrative—it will cast doubts about whether the experience you've built is truly valuable. Here are a few examples of why you might make a lateral move:

- Transferring to a different industry or type of organization—for example, from a public to a private equity–owned company, from a for-profit to a not-for-profit organization—to expand the breadth of your experience and demonstrate that you can adapt to different environments.
- To gain international experience or utilize your capability in another language.
- To have the opportunity to work for a more prestigious organization.
- To jump from the predictability of a large, established corporation to the uncertainty and excitement of an early-stage company.

To Jump or Not to Jump (to a Start-Up)

Natalia, twenty-four, was working as a marketing manager at one of the world's largest software companies when she was offered a job at a hot new start-up that blended social media, fashion, and online shopping. The decision was tearing her apart. On one hand, it looked like an opportunity to get into something on the ground floor, have a great learning experience, and enjoy the adrenaline rush of making meaningful contributions to an early-stage company. Given the momentum of the start-up, the quality of its venture capital investors, and the proven track record of its founders, it could have been a once-in-a-lifetime chance. And if things really worked out, she could even make a lot of money.

On the other hand, Natalia had been in her current job for only thirteen months, and she felt that it was too soon to be considering a move. She was in a good job with a highly regarded company, and she was making solid money with full health benefits. She was working hard, but the hours weren't unreasonable, and the position provided her with a clear track for advancement.

If you were in Natalia's situation, which way would you lean? Or if you were helping a friend confronting this decision, what would you tell him or her? To see the situation more clearly, you might start by considering the many reasons for joining a start-up.

I Could Make a Ton of Money

There are many good reasons to join a start-up—but money really shouldn't be one of them. The media and movies are full of stories about people who got in on the ground floor of a start-up and made millions, but the fact is that most start-ups fail, even those that are most hyped. According to research by Shikhar Ghosh, a senior lecturer at Harvard Business School, approximately three out of four start-ups fail. For every

Google, there were hundreds of close competitors that bit the dust. For every Facebook, there were countless other social networks that were well funded and poised to succeed, but didn't. Venture capitalists' portfolios are typically composed of dozens of companies that don't make it and one or two investments that hit it big. For venture capitalists, the returns from their hits compensate for the losses from the rest—but in your career you get to work at only one company at a time, so you may want to think about the odds a little differently. Unless you are fortunate enough to choose one of the few start-ups that hits it big, you will probably not make as much money as you would at a large company.

Let's look at the math. Assume you make an average of $75,000 a year for the next three years at a large company along with full benefits. All told, that's worth about $85,000 a year, or $255,000 in three-year pretax income. As a comparison, let's assume you join a start-up with an entry-level salary that will typically be on the order of $30,000 and some options at the company's current valuation, which let's set at $50 million. Now, bearing in mind the research that 75 percent of start-ups fail, consider three potential outcomes:

- *Start-up A: Google/Facebook-like success.* The company has a massive IPO; let's optimistically set the probability of a $10 billion valuation at 5 percent.
- *Start-up B: Moderate success.* The company does reasonably well in the market but doesn't meet its growth projections or achieve a suc-

cessful IPO; let's set the probability of the company being acquired for double the valuation, or $100 million, at 20 percent.

- *Start-up C: Failure.* The company doesn't make it and the options never materialize; the probability of this is, in fact, approximately 75 percent.

Your three years of cash from the start-up will be $90,000. The question is, how many options would you have to be granted to make up for the $165,000 of higher cash and benefits from the large company *on a risk-adjusted basis*? The answer is you'd need a grant of approximately 0.3 percent of the start-up. This is actually a fairly typical grant if you are one of the first fifty or one hundred employees of a company and you are in the early days of your career. If you are lucky enough to jump to a start-up in which scenario A plays out, you'll make $3 million from your 0.3 percent options grant (actually it would more likely be $1.5 million, assuming the company had to raise more equity prior to the IPO, diminishing your stake by half). If scenario B unfolded, you could make about $15,000 from your options. So on a risk-adjusted basis, on the basis of the assumptions above, this 0.3 percent grant plus the $30,000 annual salary would be worth about the same as the $255,000 in three-year compensation from the large company.

If you're deciding whether to jump to a start-up company, it's critical to work through the numbers. It's natural to be excited at the prospect of making millions, but keep the probabilities in mind, recognizing that even with the successes, most of the money goes to the founders and the venture capitalists who funded the company and own the most shares.

It's a Once-in-a-Lifetime Chance

This might be true. You might never get a chance to take a risk like this again. As you grow older and advance in your career, you might not be as willing to embrace risk like this. You'll have more obligations, such as a spouse, children, or a mortgage, and you might not be ready to devote your nights and weekends to the start-up's success.

Consequently, this is one of the soundest reasons for jumping to a start-up early in your career. In Natalia's case, she would have plenty of time to recover and move forward if the social media, fashion, and online shopping start-up failed a year after she joined. If you're like her and have an adventurous disposition, you might be happy taking a risk like hers early on in your professional life.

I Want to Start a Company One Day, So I Want to Learn How It Works

This is another good reason to join a start-up. But a word of caution: many people find that unless they are one of the first half-dozen employees to join, they actually don't learn much about how to start a company of their own. The main thing they do develop is a sense of what a start-up *feels* like from the inside, and the ability to differentiate between a company poised for success and a company that's on life support.

I Love Having the Sense That I'm Building Something, and I Want to Figure Out If a Start-Up Environment Suits Me Better Than That of a Big Corporation

Company culture is important, so it is valuable to test out different environments so you can determine the best fit for you. Just the same, it's important to consider the role in which you would be working at a start-up. While any job can be fun and exciting for a time, you don't want to ignore the skill set you will spend time developing in your position. You might find that a start-up offers you the opportunity to be more stretched by having to do more with fewer resources. You might be given responsibilities for designing products, selling the company's services, hiring people, or trying to do deals at the early-stage company years ahead of when you might be given that chance at a large corporation. The potential for garnering these experiences needs to be balanced by the quality of the people and processes at the start-up versus the large company. Where are you more likely to build a stronger foundation of skills and experiences? As we explored in chapter 1, The Six Phases of Your Career, an important priority in the Aspiration and Promise phases is experimenting with a variety of areas, company types, and roles before settling into your chosen path.

As with all decisions, it's impossible to be 100 percent sure about whether or not to join a start-up. But hopefully, this analysis will help you to break the big question into smaller ones and arrive at a decision that is right for you. There is no shortage of interesting start-ups, especially in today's economy—but before joining one, you should really kick the tires on the company, think through the job you would be doing, and assess the quality of the culture and the people involved. If you are truly blown away, then go for it. But if you jump in, make sure to do so with eyes wide open.

For the record, Natalia ended up deciding to stay in her marketing manager job at the large company for the time being. As of the time of this writing, the start-up she almost joined is doing okay, likely to end up in category B, moderate success.

13

NEGOTIATING (OR NOT) TO GET MORE MONEY

One of the trickiest aspects of managing your career is knowing when and how to negotiate for a raise in your current job or a higher salary offer in a new position. As we discussed in chapter 3, What About Money?, there are generally two types of people: those for whom money is the primary goal of their career and those for whom it plays an important but supporting role. No matter which camp you're in, you will almost certainly wonder at some point in your career, *Should I ask for more money?* You know that if you don't ask, you probably won't receive it; but if you mishandle the ask, you risk blowing an offer or creating an adversarial relationship on the job.

This is one of the most delicate issues in career management. Handle with extreme caution.

How to Negotiate (or Not) When You're *Offered* a Job

"Great news!" the e-mail from Andrew to me began. "I got the offer to become Associate Creative Director, and I'm super excited. I am going to accept. That being said, the salary they've offered is a little low. It's not offensively low, and it's within the realm of what's appropriate for the position. But I'd like to try and negotiate it up a little, from $70,000 to around $77,500. Any suggestions? It's tough to not just jump in and take the initial offer, but I wondered if you might have some advice."

A job offer puts you in an exciting but delicate position. The stakes are high, and you'll probably be pressed for time. You're uncertain about what will happen if you push for a better salary. But six months down the road, will you wish that you hadn't left that money on the table? How should you respond?

First of all, express your appreciation and excitement for having received the offer. You've worked hard to get this far, and so has the employer. Express your enthusiasm for the opportunity, and if you are planning to accept don't play hard to get. Make it clear that you would like to accept but that before you do you would like to discuss the offer. Have this conversation by phone, not over e-mail. If possible, offer to come to the office and talk it through in person.

Next, do some homework:

- See if you can get any information about the salaries of associate creative directors at comparable companies.

- Is there anyone that you met in the interview process who could tell you the salary range for a comparable position in their organization?
- Can you find information about the position's compensation on social media, or on websites like Glassdoor?
- Do you know anyone from college or graduate school who has worked in a similar role?
- Do you know anyone inside the organization but outside the hiring area who can tell you how compensation works at the organization?

Finally, when it comes time to have the conversation with your prospective employer, make sure to strike an enthusiastic and respectful tone while being honest that your financial needs are slightly higher than what was offered. Find a justification that can anchor your request, something like:

- Before graduate school, when I worked as a freelancer, my annualized rate of compensation was $65,000.
- My compensation in my current job is $68,000 and I think a 10 percent increase is appropriate given the risk I'm taking to move companies and given the breadth of the job.
- My understanding is that associate creative director positions at other comparable companies range from $70,000 to $100,000.
- How does this salary compare with other positions in the organization? What is the range of compensation among all the associate creative directors?

- When I model my financial needs—especially considering my student loans from grad school—I really could use a somewhat higher amount.

If the employer asks you for a specific number, suggest a small range that's slightly above your actual need (in this case, you would say $78,000 to $82,500), and be willing to take the middle ground. If you get the sense that the employer doesn't want to budge on their offer, you might ask questions like these:

- What would a typical compensation path look like, starting as an associate creative director over the next three to five years, assuming outstanding performance?
- Are there opportunities for performance-based bonuses? Long-term/deferred compensation?

"What Are Your Salary Requirements?"

It is not uncommon for an employer to ask, "What are your salary requirements?" before they make an offer.

This can be a tricky situation. If you provide a number that's too low, the employer might undervalue you and question whether you are in fact the right person for the job. But if you put out an amount that strikes them as being too high, you risk offending them and giving them the impression that you're greedy.

If you're asked to name your desired salary, don't give a number unless you've really done your homework. You don't need to answer on the spot—tell the interviewer that you will run some numbers and get

right back to them. Then go home and do some research, using the questions listed above as a guide.
And if you haven't already done so, ask the employer
to explain their compensation system. What do their
top employees make, and what do junior members get
paid? At what level would you be coming in?

Handle with Care

No matter how negotiation unfolds, it is extremely important to read the situation and use all your senses
to guide the discussion. If you handle it well, you will
either get the higher compensation or at least earn respect for considering your options. Just make sure not
to be greedy or put the employer in a competitive bind.
Never feign that you have a competitive offer and are
playing one off against another. That is a high-risk
strategy, even if you *have* received an offer from another company.

Once an offer is made, the employer will be in a
vulnerable position. The power dynamic has shifted
to one in which you now have the power to turn *them*
down. Even if there's a backup candidate, the employer
will have gotten all its internal approvals secured before extending the offer to you. If you fall through, that
just means more work for them, and it could be embar-
rassing for the people who signed off on hiring you. In
other words, the company is as worried as you are about
how the situation will turn out.

So, if you're offered a job, treat the situation with
care. The grace with which you conduct the discussions

in this emotionally charged scenario will create an enduring impression about your attitudes and professionalism.

Negotiating (or Not) When *on* the Job

Once you're on the job, it can be difficult to break out of the company's standard process for increasing your compensation. But at some point you may well feel that you've earned a raise. How can you act on this feeling while minimizing the risk of harming your relationship with your boss or giving your coworkers the impression that you are greedy? Here are five steps for earning and negotiating a raise, in the short or medium term:

Step 1: Deserve a Raise

If you want a raise, the most important thing you can do is deserve one. Companies are under relentless pressure to satisfy the demands of their stakeholders, and this means they must strive to achieve increased profitability, quarter after quarter—and employees' salaries go directly to that bottom line.

Most people think they themselves are performing well at work, but the obvious fact is that some contribute more to the organization's success. So do your best to make yourself essential to the enterprise. It is incumbent upon you to know exactly how your work fits into the company's strategy for creating and capturing value. If you don't know, find out—and if you discover that your project is on the periphery, find a way to get involved in something more central to the company's efforts.

Once you're sure you're working on and excelling in the right kinds of projects, follow the advice from chapters 10 and 11, Getting Off to the Right Start in a New Job and Four Guaranteed Strategies for Success. If you work hard, are a strong team player, maintain a positive attitude, and take the right amount of initiative, you will be well positioned to negotiate for a raise.

Step 2: Get the Facts

It's your responsibility to know your market value and understand how your compensation compares to that of people in comparable roles. To find this, talk to your organization's human resources department to understand the pay scales in your company, as well as the companies they compare themselves to when setting pay for your position. If your HR department won't share that information with you, speak to friends, mentors, your college's career services center, and people working in similar jobs in other organizations.

You can also take advantage of information available publicly on the Internet. At no point in history has so much salary information been as easy to get as it is today. Be cautious, however, in using the data coming back from Internet searches. Different companies, industries, cities, and regions have their own unique compensation structures, so take the time to make distinctions based on industry, organization size, job function, geography, and required level of education and training. Find databases that are trustworthy and used widely. LinkedIn's Salary Expectation Calculator is a good place to start, and Success Factors, Salary.com, and Moving.com are other sites where you can find helpful salary information.

Step 3: Talk to Your Boss

Now you're ready to initiate that delicate conversation with your boss. As I stressed above, it's important to be sensitive when discussing your compensation. It's well known that managers are anxious when giving performance reviews, and they find compensation discussions to be just as stressful. So make sure to approach this talk in a constructive manner. Put the conversation into a broader context by assessing your performance in a way that shows how it fits into your department's strategy. Solicit feedback. Share your findings from step 2, and ask what your boss thinks your expectations for compensation should be. Don't be pushy, and don't ask directly for more money, but be clear that compensation is an important part of the overall equation for you.

In addition to your compensation, communicate the other facets of your job that you value, such as being able to contribute to the company's strategy, working with people you respect and enjoy, and being provided with chances to learn and grow. Your boss will almost certainly respond better when compensation is one of the items on a broader, more holistic list.

Step 4: Offer to Take on a Special Project

If your compensation is locked in for the year, or if your boss says his or her hands are tied by budgetary constraints, another approach is to suggest that you lead a special project for the company. Assuming that you fully understand how your job and contributions fit into your department's strategy, you should be able to devise a viable effort that would be well received. Examples include offering to help lead college recruiting for your organization, hosting a training seminar for other early-career employees, doing a special intellectual capital project to market your company's services, or performing a competitive or market study. Suggest to your boss that you lead this special project and that, if it's successful, you receive a special performance bonus for your work.

Step 5: If All Else Fails

If you've followed all these steps and still find yourself up against a brick wall, it may be time to make a change. If your salary is non-negotiable, if there are no opportunities for performance bonuses, and if your market intelligence tells you that you're undercompensated, it may be time to consider looking outside the organization for a new job.

Hopefully, there won't be too many times in your career when you feel the need to negotiate for better compensation. Ideally, you will be in a position where your performance speaks for itself—where you're adding so much value that your organization decides to do the hard work of figuring out how to reward you and make you happy. If you are truly fortunate, others will be prepared to lobby on your behalf. But sometimes, of course, you need to make things happen yourself. Just make sure you approach those situations with care.

HOW TO CULTIVATE A MENTOR

Benjamin Franklin's story is a perfect example of how valuable mentors can be for your professional success and personal satisfaction. In 1727, at age twenty-one, the young Franklin formed a "club of mutual improvement" that he called the Junto (based on the Spanish word for "to join"), which met at a tavern every Friday evening to discuss a wide range of issues having to do with "Morals, Politics, or Natural Philosophy." Franklin cleverly populated the group with eleven other highly experienced tradesmen (including a prominent printer, a surveyor, a mathematician, and a merchant clerk) who could help him advance in his career. Before each meeting, Franklin circulated a wide-ranging list of discussion questions, covering general interest topics and issues like "Do you think of anything at present, in which the Junto may be serviceable to mankind?" and "Do you know of any deserving young beginner lately set up, whom it lies in the power of the Junto any way to encourage?" They also focused on how to advance professionally, with such questions as "Have you lately heard how any present rich man, here or elsewhere, got his estate?" Beyond helping one another succeed, the group shared a commitment to lifelong learning. Soon the members traded books, and from the Junto the first lending library was established in the American colonies.

A mentor is someone who invests time and energy in your success. He or she imparts war stories and experiences and serves as a sounding board when you are confronting a difficult decision. The very best mentors go beyond providing advice and become advocates. They serve as a source of new business introductions, connect you with new career opportunities, and act as references when you are a candidate for a new job. A mentor is clearly key to powering you in your career. The purpose of this chapter is to show you how to cultivate one so that, like Ben Franklin, you don't have to go it alone.

Strauss Zelnick is founder and managing partner of Zelnick Media, a private equity firm. He's also a particularly devoted mentor. Over the last twenty years, Strauss has advised more than a thousand young professionals in their careers—even going so far as to actively seek out ambitious, curious young people whom he can mentor. Because of these efforts, he has developed a loyal following in his industry and has accelerated the careers of many young media executives and venture capitalists.

"When I first started working," Strauss said, "it had been so hard for me to find people willing to help that I vowed always to be available to anyone who wanted or needed advice or assistance. Over time, I've developed the belief that serving others is perhaps the best route to a good life."

Dennis Woodside, COO of Dropbox, is similarly devoted to mentorship, and he has well-developed thoughts on how mentor relationships are best sparked. "One of my mentees sought me out because she thought my personal experience, working outside the U.S. and returning to corporate headquarters, made me uniquely qualified to offer her a valuable point of view," he said. "She had a precise question about moving internationally and was incredibly persistent in trying to get my attention." He now speaks to her regularly and has come to take pride in her accelerating career success.

Many mentorships are formed in this way, when a specific question leads to meaningful dialogue and an organic relationship ensues. Other times a junior employee is assigned to work on a project with a senior colleague and slowly and steadily begins to solicit advice and build trust based on the quality of his or her work. Sometimes, as I discussed in chapter 4, The Power of Relationships and Networks, a young professional will find a way to complete a onetime project for someone outside his or her organization, using that engagement as an opportunity to form a longer-term relationship.

The Importance of Mentors

In order to thrive in your career, you'll need to lean on the help of others—whether for gaining access to opportunities or getting advice on difficult questions about what you should do or how to do it. Also, it is important to have someone else to advocate for you from time to time when it comes to decisions others will make that will affect your livelihood—securing a plum assignment, earning a promotion, being awarded a raise. These activities go beyond mentorship and into sponsorship, which links advice with tangible action on your behalf. In her book *Lean In for Graduates*, Sheryl Sandberg stresses sponsorship's crucial role in career advancement. "Men and women with sponsors are more likely to ask for stretch assignments and pay raises than their peers of the same gender without sponsors," she writes.

Alec Ross, whom we met earlier in the chapter about the liberal arts, puts it this way: "There are no self-made men or women. Whatever we achieve, we achieve in no small measure because others have chosen to care about our careers and well-being—so it is essential to understand the science and art of cultivating relationships with mentors."

THINK LIKE A SOFTWARE ENGINEER
TO CULTIVATE MENTORS

Daniel Loeb is the founder and CEO of Third Point LLC, a high-profile investment firm that takes significant positions in companies where they "anticipate a catalyst will unlock value." Since its founding in 1995, Third Point has invested in hundreds of companies, such as Yahoo!, Sony, and Sotheby's. One of Dan's signature tactics is to write eloquent, hard-hitting, well-researched letters that call for companies' boards and management teams to change. His letters, often highly publicized, are known for giving voice to how many other investors feel.

Something less widely known about Dan is that he's a devoted mentor. "I grew up in the industry with mentors," he said. "We got together and shot the breeze and in the process I learned a lot about how things are done." But Dan's views about the importance of mentors, shaped by his experience working with young entrepreneurs, have evolved since his own early days. "How is it that many of these smart young founders, like Travis Kalanick at Uber, Carter Cleveland of Artsy, and Kevin Systrom at Instagram, learn how to become outstanding business leaders?" he asks. "All have subjected themselves to mentorship," he answers. "The first thing they did was acknowledge that they needed to learn. The second thing was figuring out where they had gaps and developing mentors to help." Dan's advice to young people about mentorship is to think like software engineers. "These guys have created architectures for their businesses and defined systematically the most important gaps—whether talent and recruiting, organizational design, board governance, or financial management—and then have found the best advisers to help fill that gap."

What Mentors Are Looking For

"I always wonder what makes people decide that your success is something worth investing in."
—HANNAH, TWENTY-SIX

To better understand how mentorship works, I asked more than one hundred top business leaders to tell me about whom they've mentored over time and why. Nearly nine out of ten take an active part in mentoring someone, and the attributes they look for in their mentees are very consistent:

- **Attitude.** Are you positive and upbeat? Do you create energy when interacting with others? Do you have a "No task is too small" mindset? A good attitude is the single most common thing mentors look for when deciding who to advise.
- **Confidence.** Do you communicate with conviction when talking with senior people? Do you have opinions, and can you articulate them confidently without coming across as arrogant?
- **Curiosity.** Do you ask good questions? Are you eager to learn more? Do your questions have to do with specific issues that the mentor understands?

- **Results Orientation.** Do you take action, make things happen, and follow up on leads and introductions? Do you make solid progress on goals when no one is supervising you or telling you what to do? Do you take ownership for your results? (This is especially important if you work in the same organization as your mentor.)

- **Listening.** Are you a good listener? Do you synthesize instructions and feedback and come away with action steps?

- **Versatility.** If someone throws you into an unfamiliar problem, can you figure out a solution as you go along?

- **Respect for Time.** Do you keep in touch with the right degree of frequency and communicate on the right topics? Are you forceful and persistent about getting on the calendar at the right times?

"I look for mentees who have insatiable curiosity, are action oriented, and conscientious; when they see something broken they fix or improve it, even if it falls outside their job description."

—LASZLO BOCK, SENIOR VICE PRESIDENT
OF PEOPLE OPERATIONS, GOOGLE

What Makes a Good Mentor?

> "There are two people I consider to be my mentors, in-sofar as they have always made themselves available to me for any important professional or even personal issue. They were the first women in my chosen field who I ever met and thought, 'That is the kind of person I want to be.' That's not easy to find when you're twenty years old and someone in their thirties might as well be one hundred."
>
> **—ALEX, TWENTY-SEVEN**

We also asked thousands of young professionals about their experience with mentorship. On the basis of our results, the quality of young people's mentorship experiences varies widely:

Young Professionals: Do you have a mentor?	Frequency (%)
Yes, and he/she is very helpful	46%
Yes, but he/she doesn't really do much	15%
No, I don't have a mentor	39%

These results underscore an important point: *It can be tricky to cultivate an effective mentor relationship.* If you are too direct about asking for mentorship, you may be rebuffed and become discouraged. Or you may find that your mentor is eager to help but doesn't answer your questions in a way that gives you steps for action. Or perhaps you just haven't found someone you connect with. Whatever the reason, it is worthwhile to overcome these obstacles and work hard to find a mentor who can help you move forward in your career.

What becomes clear from our research is that young professionals and business leaders agree as to what constitutes an effective mentor relationship. It is all about honest feedback, accessibility, encouragement, and support for professional and personal goals.

Qualities/Attributes*	Young Professionals	Business Leaders
Mentor provides honest and constructive feedback (Mentee is receptive to honest feedback)	97%	97%
Mentor is accessible and available (Mentee is responsive and available)	92%	69%
Mentor is encouraging and motivational (Mentee is upbeat and enthusiastic)	90%	89%
Mentor provides valuable introductions (Mentee follows up on valuable introductions)	80%	94%

Mentor is well respected and well known by your other colleagues (Mentee is highly regarded in the organization)	70%	63%
Mentor values learning from *you* (Mentee enables *you* to learn from them)	66%	71%
Mentor/mentee meets with you in person on a regular basis	60%	51%
Mentor/mentee shares personal interests	58%	23%
*"Strongly agreed" or "agreed" as to what qualities/attributes are important in a mentor/mentee.		

Malcolm Gladwell, who mentors a number of upcoming writers, says his goal as a mentor is to be a source of encouragement. "I remind them that a lot of things they think are unattainable are actually attainable. To aspiring writers I say, *The New Yorker* is written by people like you. They may have gotten a break along the way or worked harder, but it's more a matter of your own energy, creativity, attitude, than anything else. My goal is to demystify all the worlds that I'm in that other people want to get into."

Our survey results also indicate that mentorship ideally is a two-way relationship. Mentors receive both tangible and important psychic benefits from the relationship. On the tangible side, your mentor wants to learn from you, often about the views of younger people, or frequently about technology and social media. On the less tangible side, mentors report that they get a sense of pride and fulfillment from investing in the success of talented up-and-comers. So, if you're developing a mentor, make sure to think about what they might be getting from the relationship.

> "Every mentor needs to understand that students looking for a job and starting off in their careers are continually flipping out, all the time. Every day that their fates remain unknown, they are spiraling into negative places, and consider every unknown minute a step towards rejection."
>
> **—NICKI, TWENTY-THREE**

How to and *How Not to* Cultivate a Mentor Relationship

Although many organizations have programs for connecting young employees with mentors, *effective* mentorship is not usually mediated through an official program. Mentorship at its best is a voluntary activity, and the relationship is one that develops naturally over time.

Also, don't think that you need to commit to a single mentor. It is wise to cultivate several trusted advisory relationships with individuals who have complementary experiences—for example, people from both inside and outside your organization, or from different locations or functional areas.

Cultivating a Mentor/ Mentee Relationship	Young Professionals		Business Leaders	
	Yes	No	Yes	No
The relationship developed naturally over time	75%	25%	95%	5%
Mentee worked hard to get advice	52%	48%	18%	82%
Mentee thanked mentor for spending time and then one thing led to another	50%	50%	79%	21%
This person was assigned to me at work	25%	75%	24%	76%

The most sure-fire way to fail in cultivating a mentor is to ask someone, literally, "Will you be my mentor?" In most cases, it's not wise to force the relationship or put a label on it. When Sheryl Sandberg gives a speech or meets with a large gathering of people, often someone will come up to her afterward and ask her to be their mentor. It's "a total mood killer," she says. "While flattering, the interaction is awkward."

A better approach is to capture a prospective mentor's attention after having carefully considered how to approach him or her with a specific question or topic of conversation. "I have seen lower-level employees nimbly grab a moment after a meeting or in the hall to ask advice from a respected and busy senior person," Sheryl says. "The exchange is casual and quick. After taking that advice, the would-be mentee follows up to offer thanks and then uses that opportunity to ask for more guidance. Without even realizing it, the senior person becomes involved and invested in the junior person's career. The word *mentor* never needs to be uttered." She also adds that vague questions and questions that can be answered with a basic online search (e.g., "What is Facebook's culture like?") are a turnoff because they show a lack of ingenuity.

Mentoring in Their Own Image

Most successful people know that it is dangerous to *hire* people in their own image. But since mentorship is a voluntary activity, many business leaders tend to "mentor in their own image," even if they don't readily admit it. In observing mentors across various companies and industries, I've noticed that mentors often see themselves in their mentees, and academic research confirms this intuition. A study published in the *Journal of Vocational Behavior* found that mentor and sponsor relationships are frequently grounded in shared interests, personalities, and career values.

Common interests can be a powerful way to establish and strengthen the relationship bond. I've overheard mentors talking with young people about anything from organic food, to what school each person attended, to recent movies, modern art, sports, or singing a capella. Often, when the bond becomes stronger, mentees will begin to mimic some of their mentors' behaviors— their tone of voice, their words or expressions, or the way they sign their e-mails. The mimicry can even extend to more big-picture characteristics, like their leadership style, the kind of assignments they take on, even the way they dress. The point here is that a valuable mentor is often someone who demonstrates habits and characteristics that you could see yourself coming to emulate.

When I interviewed Sheryl Sandberg for this book, she urged me to not shy away from the topic of gender, "even though it may be charged, and if it is more difficult for you because you are a guy." Sheryl's advice illuminates a very real phenomenon. Since people tend to mentor in their own image, men often choose to mentor younger men, and women tend to seek advice and mentorship from successful women. There is nothing wrong with this on its own, but because men are better represented in the highest levels of most organizations and industries, young women can be at a disadvantage when it comes to cultivating influential mentors who can help them in their careers. The solution, Sheryl says, is to "make male leaders aware of this shortage and encourage them to widen their circle." Ideally, this will lead to action. "It's wonderful when senior men mentor women," Sheryl says. "It's even better when they champion and sponsor them."

─⊖─

If this exploration of mentorship sounds familiar by this point in the book, that shouldn't be a surprise. The key themes of how to think about your career, how to get a good job, and how to thrive are consistent and interrelated, and they work. They have everything to do with maintaining a genuinely positive attitude, working really hard, being curious, versatile, and persistent, developing strong relationships, communicating well, and thinking about how you can support others.

CONCLUSION

Onward to Success and Happiness

Ted Leonsis is a serial entrepreneur who in 1994 sold his company to America Online (AOL) and stayed with the company for thirteen years as vice chairman and president of its audience group. Today he owns a number of professional sports teams, including the NHL's Washington Capitals and the WNBA's Washington Mystics, and he partly owns the NBA's Washington Wizards. Ted is also chairman of Groupon and a member of American Express's board. In other words, he's a professional success, any way you slice it.

When Ted was twenty-seven, he was on a routine flight from Florida to Atlanta when suddenly the pilot came over the intercom and told the passengers to prepare for a crash landing. The plane's landing gear had malfunctioned, and the pilot was ordered to circle the airport and burn off fuel before attempting to land in order to reduce the amount of explosive fuel on board. It was during these thirty-five terrifying minutes of preparation that Ted had a depressing epiphany. By this point in his life, Ted, who had already founded, built, and sold his first technology company, had already had his first taste of real success. But he realized that if he died in the crash he would die as an unhappy person who had focused on work at the expense of everything else that was truly important. In that moment, Ted made a vow that if he made it out of this alive, he would change his priorities and do a better job of living.

Fortunately, the plane made a safe emergency landing, and a few days later Ted began working to fulfill his end of the bargain he had made during the harrowing flight. He began a "Life List" of all the things he wanted to experience and achieve in his life—both inside and outside his career. Ted has kept his list handy through the years, and each time he completes one of the goals he checks it off. The list, which we'll discuss in detail later in this chapter, has helped Ted to keep himself accountable for taking time to do things that make him happy.

I want to conclude *The Career Playbook* by talking about the relationship between success and happiness. I hope this book has provided you with a number of principles, strategies, and tactics for achieving success in your professional life. I believe that if you apply them thoughtfully and rigorously, you will be able to set a sound direction for your career and land a good job that will enable you to thrive. I have every confidence that you now have the tools to succeed in your career, both in the coming seasons and over the long term.

But I haven't written as much about happiness, and it's worth spending a few pages on this important but surprisingly complex topic. Paul Dolan, a renowned behavioral scientist at the London School of Economics, has come to believe that the pursuit of happiness is the very aim of human existence. In his book *Happiness by Design*, he defines happiness in a way that makes a great deal of sense to me:

> "Happiness is the experience of both pleasure and purpose over time."
> **—PAUL DOLAN**

I love this definition. On the one hand, it captures the sense of achievement that you get from challenging but meaningful endeavors—projects that move things forward, breakthrough ideas, and products, deals that satisfy clients, and work that helps those in need. But Dolan's definition of happiness also encompasses a wide range of activities that bring you joy, even if their outcomes don't always produce measurable results—activities such as listening to music, creating art, watching films, playing sports, enjoying the great outdoors, and spending time with the people you love. Some activities, the ones you want to maximize, are high on both pleasure and purpose. Others are high on one of the two and are worth doing, with some degree of moderation. Finally, there are activities that are painful to experience, that do not contribute to something meaningful, and that bring you neither joy nor meaning. These, of course, are the ones you want to avoid at all costs.[1]

---

[1] I do not put an entry-level job, even if it requires starting out at the bottom, into this category. Even if it is painful and seemingly without purpose, you have the opportunity to take that experience and have it contribute meaningfully to building your career.

The Relationship Between Success and Happiness

Many people believe that the greater your career success, the greater your happiness. Others might not agree with this statement outright, but they nevertheless organize their lives so that most of their time and energy is spent pursuing success. In this paradigm, the relationship between success and happiness is captured by an upwardly sloping curve.

CAREER SUCCESS AND HAPPINESS

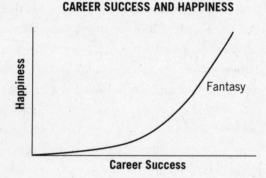

It's certainly true that career success often leads to happiness and a sense of fulfillment—but the relationship is not as straightforward as many people think. Research shows that after a certain level of professional success, obtaining more money, power, and prestige results in diminishing returns in terms of your happiness.

The true relationship between success and happiness can be better expressed by an inverted U-curve. Beyond a certain baseline level of material success, happiness falls as your level of success rises.

Why is this often the case? The greater your suc-

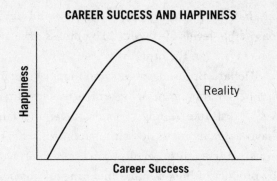

CAREER SUCCESS AND HAPPINESS

cess, the more responsibilities you have, and the more things there are that will vie for your attention. You'll be managing people who have their own hopes and dreams. You'll have to attend more meetings and have less time for yourself. You'll have investments to manage, and you'll probably have a spouse and kids who will need your attention when you come home from a stressful day at the office. These, of course, are all good things in themselves—but they do make your life more complicated.

Because of this, it is worth asking two questions about the relationship between success and happiness. The first has to do with causality. Does success lead to happiness, or does happiness lead to success? Which is the chicken and which is the egg? Unless you stop to really think about it, the tendency is to act as if success were the independent variable that will bring you the dependent variable: happiness.

But causality may well run in the other direction. Ted Leonsis certainly came to think so when his plane almost crashed to the ground. Ever since his near-death experience, Ted has built his life and career on the notion that, by pursuing *happiness*, he could achieve unimaginable levels of success. "Happiness drives success," he says, "not the other way around."

For Richard Branson, success and money contribute to happiness, but happiness, for him, is the primary objective. "Words like 'family,' 'friends,' 'love,' and 'laughter' have a lot more to do with happiness," he says, "than words like 'gross,' 'capital,' and 'revenue.' Money is a by-product of bigger, more meaningful goals such as passion, fun, and wisdom. My approach is to have fun, do good, and the money will come."

If you buy into this logic, there are two approaches you can take to actively pursue happiness. But before turning to them, let's revisit the second part of the relationship between success and happiness: proportionality, or the fact that as with ice cream, leisure time, or fame, more is not necessarily better when it comes to success.

Malcolm Gladwell offers this explanation. "The irony is that you often don't understand the relationship between success and happiness until it's too late. Some things you can understand in the moment, but the implications of setting your goal to maximize career success are in that category of life lessons often not learned until after you've lived through it." In other words, focusing on career success *to the exclusion or expense of* other important things, such as deep personal relationships or deeply meaningful work, is a well-trodden road to unhappiness.

How to Pursue Happiness

There are two concrete steps you can take to pursue happiness. The first comes from Paul Dolan. He suggests that you start a daily log of your experiences and activities and rate each activity on a scale from 1 to 10, on the basis of the amounts of both pleasure and purpose it brings you. Begin logging your activities in this way, and after a few months take a step back and look at your log. How much of your time are you spending on things that rate higher than a 5 on each dimension? How much on activities that rate a 3 or less? Is there anything you can do to spend more time doing the activities that you've rated highly? What activities are you *not* currently doing that you would rate highly if you had time to work them into your schedule?

Often our routines and activities get established not by our conscious decisions but by the people and responsibilities that constantly compete for our time and attention. If you keep a log of your daily activities, it will help you to gauge whether the life you're living is the one you want to live. And it can help you to begin shifting your efforts in the direction of things that bring you pleasure *and* purpose.

The second approach to maximizing happiness in your life and career is inspired by Ted Leonsis and his Life List. Ted advises young professionals to recognize the power of setting concrete, time-bound goals and taking the extra step of actually writing them down. It may be intimidating to think up (and commit yourself to) goals that might not be realized until later on in your life. But Ted believes this process is one of the most direct paths to happiness.

To give you a sense of what kind of goals you might articulate, here's what Ted wrote on his Life List, starting back when he was twenty-seven years old:

- **Family Matters**—Fall in love and get married. Have a healthy son. Have a healthy daughter. Take care of parents.
- **Financial**—Pay off college debts. Attain net worth of $10 million; $100 million. Have zero personal debt for family. Start a company and sell it.
- **Possessions**—Have a beach home. Own a great piece of art. Own a personal collection of watches. Restore an antique auto. Own a restaurant or club.
- **Charities**—Change someone's life via a charity. Give $1 million to Georgetown University. Sit on the board of Georgetown. Start a family charity foundation.
- **Sports**—Own a major league sports franchise. Attend a Final Four with Georgetown. Attend a World Series with the Yankees. Catch a foul ball. Go to the Olympics. Play a round of golf at Augusta National. Get a hole-in-one.
- **Travel**—Go to Greece, Italy, London, Jerusalem, Paris, Hawaii, Brazil, Alaska, China, sail through the Mediterranean, Caribbean.
- **Stuff**—Produce a TV show. Write a book. Invent a board game. Go to the White House,

Meet the President. See the Rolling Stones. Go
to the Oscars. Travel to outer space.

As you can see, Ted certainly wasn't shy when deciding what goals to commit himself to. But the point
is that he took the time to articulate what he really
wanted in his life. And while he still hasn't gone to
space or hit a hole in one, he has accomplished just
about all of the other goals from his list—goals he
firmly believes he never would have realized if he
hadn't committed them to paper. Ted also says that although the goals on his list skew heavily toward the
pleasure end of the happiness spectrum, his pursuit of
them has helped to catalyze the success he has enjoyed
in his career.

This underscores the importance of taking time
outside work to do the things you love. It is something
Guhan Selvaretnam, former SVP of Discovery Digital
Media, learned early on in his career. "Having all your
energy eggs in one basket—your career—doesn't allow
for replenishment and perspective," he says. "This can
potentially lead to an unhealthy and sometimes fatal
over-reaction to the inherent ups and downs of the
work world." Pursuing activities outside the office does
more than reinvigorate you and make you more lively
and interesting back in the office—it can often help
you develop the meaningful relationships with people
who have shared interests that lead to contentment and
satisfaction free of ulterior professional motives.

You don't have to be like Ted Leonsis, Richard
Branson, Malcolm Gladwell, or anyone else, for that

matter, to become both successful and happy. Two of the most contented young people I know are a married couple who both work at a prominent boarding school. Nicki works in admissions, Derek is a history teacher, and both coach various sports and serve as dorm parents while holding a number of other responsibilities at the school. As part of their jobs, they have an on-campus apartment and are able to enjoy the school's sports and cultural facilities. They both feel that even though they work hard they have incredibly balanced lives in which they are able to spend ample time with loved ones, work in an environment that they enjoy, and do things they love.

Success and happiness can be achieved even if you start your career in a suboptimal job after graduating from an unknown school. And whether you become a CEO, a comedy writer, a consultant, or a teacher, you can pursue those things that bring you purpose and pleasure both inside and outside your job.

Coming Full Circle

Over the time that I've been working on this book, another story of career success has been unfolding, on a more modest scale. My twenty-seven-year-old niece Alex, the illustrator, graduated and pursued many of the strategies in these pages. She was creative in pursuing opportunities, using her magazine, *Until Now*, as a vehicle to generate introductions and conversation in job interviews. She cultivated mentors, developed the skill to interview well, and was continuously reminded of the importance of relationships and networks. When she finally found an opportunity that balanced her interests, experiences, and strengths, as senior designer for *Time Out New York*, she pursued it energetically and landed the job. Alex negotiated appropriately for her compensation and got off to the right start in the job by having a positive attitude, focusing on responsiveness, communicating effectively, becoming a student of the culture, and doing high-quality work. She's still in her first year at *Time Out*, but she loves the people she's working with and feels that she is making a real difference. By bringing her creativity, leadership, and art direction skills to the magazine, Alex is helping shape how the publication looks and feels, all with the goal of delighting readers.

─⊖─

My hope is that by the time you're in your late twenties and beyond, you too will have a similar story of success to tell. As you continue on the winding road of your career, I wish you the very best of success and happiness.

Appendix A

The Latter Three Phases of Your Career

For the sake of completeness, and to lay the foundation of essential advice for aspiring *older* professionals, here is a brief review of the latter three phases of a career.

The Six Career Phases

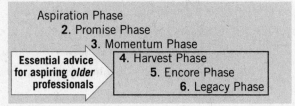

Aspiration Phase
2. Promise Phase
3. Momentum Phase

Essential advice for aspiring *older* professionals
4. Harvest Phase
5. Encore Phase
6. Legacy Phase

THE HARVEST PHASE

This phase kicks in at about your twentieth college reunion and runs for the next ten to twenty years, depending on which industry sector you're working in and how you are progressing. It is in the Harvest Phase that careers begin to diverge most dramatically. Some people manage to keep growing personally and professionally, moving into new positions or redefining their existing roles. Their careers are characterized by increasing options, more interesting alternatives, and higher compensation. For many others, however, their progress starts to slow. They get passed over for new opportunities. They may feel they are in a rut. Even though they might be doing what they have always done and continuing to do it well, their career trajectory seems to have flattened out. The key to continuing to advance through your Harvest Phase is to keep learning and find ways to convert all of your experiences into new situations. In other words, your aim is to transform the value of your experience into new potential value by finding new avenues that will value your skills and experience. Examples are the divisional president who is able to persuade a CEO search committee that his experience in one sector would be ideally suited to leading a company in another sector, the retiring CEO who becomes an operating partner in a private equity firm overseeing portfolio companies, the career accountant who is elected to corporate board directorships to chair audit committees, or the top corporate executive who mentors entrepreneurs—and maybe even becomes one him- or herself.

When you reach this stage, if you don't find a way to apply your skills and track record to new situations, essentially reinventing yourself, your value in the marketplace will inevitably and inexorably decline. The keys to navigating this phase, therefore, are to set new goals and determine how your experience and expertise can be applied to new situations. Doing this successfully will allow you to maintain your career momentum and enhance your value as well as increase your ability to have a positive impact on others. In fact, another way to think about the Harvest Phase is as the "Give Back Phase." The extraordinarily wealthy have found this to be true in The Giving Pledge. But you don't have to be a billionaire to find opportunities to give back through mentoring, getting involved in your community, and taking pleasure in trying to be a really good boss. We really do get more by giving, and this attitude can give you positive energy and focus throughout your career—but especially in the Harvest, Encore, and Legacy phases.

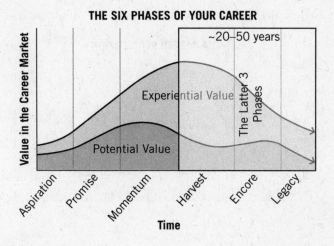

THE SIX PHASES OF YOUR CAREER

THE ENCORE PHASE

This stage follows traditional corporate retirement. It is well known that careers are not ending like clockwork at the age of sixty-five. Some people retire early and seek new interests, but others continue in their roles and organizations until well into their seventies. Others still leave the arena where they have spent the bulk of their careers and, given good health and a more active lifestyle, pursue an "encore career." Either out of desire or necessity, many people find opportunities to move into new fields of interest in the Encore Phase. A successful and meaningful Encore Phase can be characterized by remaining relevant, being sought out for advice and introductions, teaching and mentoring while simultaneously learning new skills, pursuing interests based on personal meaning, and finding ways to continue having an impact on your community and giving back.

Whether in the Harvest or the Encore Phase, if you do manage to change your direction dramatically, apply your experience to create new potential, and reinvent yourself, your career trajectory may take on a different look, more like this.

THE CAREER REINVENTION

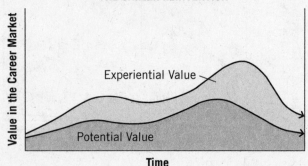

THE LEGACY PHASE

Finally, there is the Legacy Phase. You might think about this as the new age of retirement, given lengthening life spans and longer terms of employment. During this stage, you can, of course, expect to be focused on your health and your family, as well as the people and institutions that have been meaningful to you over the course of your life. This is the time for staying as physically active and mentally sharp as possible, for nurturing relationships with loved ones, for generational philanthropy, looking after your grand-children, and estate planning. As is the case for the Encore Phase, the more you can remain relevant, sought after, and respected, the more you will feel that your life and career are marked by success, meaning, and well-being.

Appendix B

How Select Colleges and Universities Are Helping Their Students Compete More Effectively

The challenge of leveraging your liberal arts education into a successful career is not solely up to you, the student or recent graduate, to solve. Colleges and universities are having to respond in order to compete, as they face pressure to justify their costs and ensure the effectiveness of their career services departments. We asked career center directors from leading schools—Dartmouth, Indiana, Middlebury, Vassar, Wesleyan, and Colgate, among numerous others—how they are responding to the challenge, and consistent themes and actions are emerging as to the resources and programs they are putting in place for students and young alumni.

All schools are focused on better preparing their students to enter the career marketplace. At Middlebury College, in bucolic northern Vermont, career services director Don Kjelleren is no exception. Don and his team have designed a comprehensive set of seminars, workshops, and programs to help identify alternative career paths, provide resources and education to get students up to speed and connect with alumni, and facilitate a peer mentoring network so that students can help fellow students. But even at top-ranked liberal arts schools such as Middlebury, there are real challenges facing career services programs. Often liberal arts students are not able to articulate their transferrable skills,

Don says, and they don't understand the importance of developing a narrative or how to market themselves. "They think their Middlebury degree and 3.9 GPA with a double major and involvement in extracurricular activities speaks for itself."

Stacie Hagenbaugh is the career development director at another elite liberal arts school, Smith College, in Northampton, Massachusetts. One of the most renowned all-women's colleges, Smith, founded in 1871, has been extremely aggressive in arming its students and alumni to compete in the workplace. Stacie said that 85 percent of members of the most recent graduating class at Smith have come through the Career Development Office at least once during their four years. They also report high degrees of satisfaction with the services provided. The school hosts over eighty career workshops every year and helps its students break the Permission Paradox by funding unpaid summer internships. Smith has an endowed program called Praxis, which guarantees each student with a stipend of up to $3,500 to work for one summer at an unpaid internship, relieving the economic burden to both student and employer. For the past fifteen years, approximately four hundred students annually have received Praxis stipends to work at unpaid summer internships in such fields as health care, government, education, communications, research, social welfare, technology, law, science, and the arts. These opportunities have helped students build on their studies, make decisions about their careers, and acquire the experiences sought out by employers and graduate schools. A survey of recent Praxis recipients showed that 99 percent of respondents believed that participating in the internship would make them more marketable in the future.

The winters at Colgate University, in Hamilton, New York, can be brutally cold. But things are heating up at the university's career center. Colgate recently recruited Mike Sciola as director, after having spent seventeen years at Wesleyan University, where he led the completion of a new and fully funded $10 million career center. With a campus culture that is gung-ho and engaged, Mike reports that a stunning 91 percent of Colgate *freshmen* engage with the career center. He and his team have taken a holistic view of how a liberal arts education and a career work together over the first ten years at and after Colgate. Their EMBARK program is a strategic process that starts as soon as a student arrives at school and shows what career opportunities can be offered over a student's time at Colgate and in the early years after graduation. Leveraging its loyal alumni base, the program commits enormous energy to securing Colgate-connected internships and winter shadow programs in the first and second years of a student's college experience. Then when it comes to competing for the most sought-after junior year summer internships, Colgate students have a better chance of standing out. In addition, in what is emerging as a best practice among colleges and universities, Colgate's career center is integrated into its development (i.e., fund-raising) and alumni relations department, ensuring that the school is engaging with its students and alumni holistically regarding an area they are all passionate about, careers. Partly as a result of this, Colgate has been able to raise millions of dollars for internships that support student interests not only in business but also in social causes, or what they call Careers for the Common Good.

Colleges have determined that they need to step into the breach because of how different things are today in terms of how careers are launched. In times past, you got a college education and would then go to a job where a company would invest in training you. Since organizations themselves have had to restructure and reduce costs to compete, they have in many cases eliminated entry-level training and rotational programs. Mike believes that colleges can help their students develop specific skills to complement their liberal arts education and enable them to gain a distinct advantage. Subjects such as financial literacy and knowledge management (e.g., the use and presentation of statistical information) are but two examples. "It has never been more relevant to have a liberal arts degree," Mike says, "but we need to be graduating students who are flexible, resilient, and capable of self-management of their own careers. They need to be personal entrepreneurs for the rest of their lives." He adds that his job is to introduce students to these concepts early on and to help them gain the necessary self-awareness regarding who they are, what they are good at, and where their interests lie. With that as a foundation, career services can support Colgate students and connect them with alumni and opportunities.

Sharon Belden Castonguay, Mike's successor at Wesleyan University, arrived at the Middletown, Connecticut, campus armed with an Ed.D. in human development and psychology from Harvard, and experience leading career services for MBA students at Baruch College's Zicklin School of Business. Her mandate was to take the new state-of-the-art career center and develop programs that would accelerate student career readiness and success. In her first year, she led the development of an aggressive suite of programs that have received rave early reviews. The foundation was the development of two weeklong intensive seminars. Choosing

Good Work was designed to help students identify what factors may be influencing their choice of major, internship, or career path, and to help them be mindful of their decisions and do what is right for them—regardless of the messages they may be receiving from others. CareerLab focused on personal branding and marketing a liberal arts degree to employers. Castonguay relaunched the "WEShadow Program," which created "externships" at companies and organizations led by alumni and parents for students over their winter break. In addition, alumni and recruiters in fields such as therapeutics, nonprofit, consulting, finance, medicine, law, media, and technology came to campus to be matched with students for a "speed networking" event that allowed students to practice their personal presentation skills in a low-risk setting while learning more about the options available to them. Finally, she has been focusing on reenergizing on-campus recruitment, cultivating hiring organizations to come to campus to interview students. This fall she will launch Accelerate, a job search group for seniors. Accelerate participants will commit to weekly sessions with career center staff, who will prepare candidates to compete for positions from application to offer. "We're making it easier for Wesleyan students to get step-by-step help and feedback in their search," Sharon reports. "The idea is to help scaffold seniors' efforts in real time as they navigate recruiting season."

Finally, these approaches and more are also being led by Roger Woolsey, senior assistant dean and director of the Center for Professional Development at Dartmouth College, in Hanover, New Hampshire. Roger joined Dartmouth a year ago from yet another prestigious liberal arts school, Colby College in Waterville, Maine. A marketing and advertising executive and professor at Suffolk University, Emerson College, and Boston College, Roger has always been zealous about advising, teaching, and mentoring young people over the course of his career. Often someone close to you who knows you well gives you good advice on what you should do with your career, and this was the case for Roger: his wife Susan had the idea for him to get into college career counseling. "I used to go home and complain that no one was doing anything about career development for college students, and so Susan urged me to stop talking about it and *do* something about it. Leading a career development department combines my love for academia and business development." He spent four years at Colby from 2008 to 2012 and led a rebuild of the school's career services approach. He established a four-year curriculum on careers, starting with an advisory for incoming freshmen about career principles, and then moved on to skills-based training and pragmatic tactics. At Colby, as in many elite colleges and universities, professors are typically the most influential members of the community, and the effectiveness of the career programs took off when Roger was able to integrate career planning with what transpired in the classroom. "Getting the faculty to understand the importance of career development was the key to building traction," he says.

Roger was recruited to Dartmouth in 2012 because even the prestigious Ivy League college knew the world had changed and believed it needed to overhaul its career programs. "There is an exigency with liberal arts colleges," Roger stresses, "that needs to be addressed. Tuition and other expenses are continuing to go up, and this places an enormous burden on parents and students. At the same time, at many leading colleges there is little to no trust among traditionalists on the faculty or in the administration about anything connected to helping students with their careers. Things related to career planning and preparedness are often seen as vocational and contradictory to the theory and values of liberal arts and humanities." Roger believes that a key part of the solution is to allow career development offices the freedom to work with students in a complementary way with their classroom learning and find ways to integrate academic, personal, and professional development. As he learned at Colby, the more that faculty support and participate in career development mentoring, the more effective it will be for students—and for the career development office. Roger has been actively recruiting members of the Dartmouth faculty to partner with his career advisers in support of students. And he goes one step further. "We try not to make our students come to our office," Roger says, bringing a customer service mind-set to career planning services. "We'll go see them where they are on their turf."

What do companies suggest for how college career centers can help? Laura Chambers, head of University Programs at eBay Inc., says that she is positively biased toward liberal arts candidates. She majored in history and philosophy for her own undergraduate arts degree, along with economics and international business for her companion undergraduate business degree. "I found that the skills I learned in my arts degree," she says, "have been the most useful and distinctive throughout my career." Laura was a consultant at McKinsey and then moved to strategy, marketing, and general management roles at eBay, Skype, and PayPal before taking on eBay Inc.'s campus recruiting efforts. She believes these programs being pursued by liberal arts career centers are essential for helping their students to get the best jobs.

She advises career development offices to set up internship programs directly with companies where the school's
graduates can work on relevant projects and gain demon-
strable experience. "I would draw on passionate alumni to
set up internships within their business units, potentially
even leveraging the co-op approach that some schools such
as Northeastern University and University of Waterloo do
so well for their graduates," she says. Similar to Smith, but
more directed to linking their students with posts in business, is Claremont McKenna College, which Laura singles
out for providing a full-service co-op program that works for
students and companies. The school hand-picks a number
of top students, then actively shops them around companies
where the school has established relationships, and then
goes above and beyond by providing accommodations, support, and even social activities over the summer so that the
companies don't have to carry the load.

Other players are coming onto the scene and partnering with colleges and universities to help bridge the gap between the talents, promise, desire, and potential of liberal
arts students and the pragmatic needs of employers. Koru is
a start-up company based in Seattle, Washington, that has
developed a new model to help students and help employers, and in so doing build a valuable new enterprise. The
company was founded in the spring of 2013 by entrepreneur
Kristen Hamilton on the basis of the simple value proposi-
tion of figuring out a better and more actionable way of
connecting college students and graduates to employers. She
had the notion that creating a system to complement all that
was great about a traditional college experience with real-
world work experience in innovative companies would be a
valuable mission worth pursuing.

Kristen, who had prior experience cofounding an e-commerce company and working as COO of the global not-for-profit World Learning, teamed up with Josh Jarrett, who had spent seven years leading the Gates Foundation's work in higher education innovation. Together they developed an experiential education program and recruited leading liberal arts colleges and forward-looking companies as founding partners to create what now is Koru.

Koru's college partners include such elite liberal arts colleges as Vassar, Williams, Pomona, Occidental, Connecticut College, Bates, Colorado College, Mount Holyoke, Dennison, and Whitman, and universities including Brown, Georgetown, and the University of Southern California. Their employer partners include a roster of rapidly growing and mission-driven companies such as REI, Zulily, Smartsheet, Simplicity Consulting, PayScale, Julep, Moz, and Trupanion, as well as a soon-to-be-named major Bay Area company.

The way it works is that students apply for two- to four-week intensive projects that are underwritten by specific employers. The cost is not insignificant, about $2,500. Some of the colleges are supporting applicants by providing scholarships to underwrite the cost. Over the course of the program, participants work on a defined, real-life business problem with an actively hiring company. Koru surrounds the students with coaches and mentors who are dedicated to helping them operate effectively from day one. Over the weeks they are also focused on helping the participants find a job that's a good fit.

Kristen believes the best way to learn any skill is to roll up your sleeves and do it. She says, "As a student, you try your best to avoid failure, but what catapults professional's ahead in their careers is learning from mistakes, and failing fast and cheap." Koru tries to pack months of experience into a few weeks by pushing participants to take initiative and receive detailed and actionable feedback. "You do real work, make real mistakes, and learn how to nail it next time," she says, "all in a supportive environment with peers and pros." The Koru premise and promise is not just about helping students and recent graduates get jobs but about actually helping companies improve their hiring decisions. While it is still early days, Kristen says that "our program and outcomes hold the promise that employers will have a better signal than they have today—degree + GPA—when hiring entry-level employees."

Whether Koru will become an enduring solution to bridging the gap between a liberal arts college education and a successful meaningful career remains to be seen. But the premise is absolutely sound. It's another way to overcome the Permission Paradox by attempting to take on the problem at scale and by linking insight with action as a market maker.

Sources

INTRODUCTION

Casti, Taylor. "The 31 Startups Twitter Has Acquired." *Mashable*, September 18, 2013.

Citrin, James M. "Discovering Your Route to an Extraordinary Career." Influencer Post. *LinkedIn Blog*, May 14, 2014.

Indvik, Lauren. "The 20 Startups Marissa Mayer Has Acquired at Yahoo." *Mashable*, July 31, 2013.

Lorin, Janet, and Jeanna Smialek. "College Graduates Struggle to Find Employment Worth a Degree." *Bloomberg Businessweek*, June 5, 2014.

Matthews, Steve, and Jeanna Smialek. "Recession Graduates Fretting with Lower Pay as U.S. Mends." *Bloomberg Businessweek*, July 23, 2014.

McWhinnie, Eric. "College Grads: Overqualified and Underprepared?" *USA Today*, May 24, 2013.

Schuckies, Erica. "What Millennials Really Want." *LinkedIn Today*, July 24, 2014.

CHAPTER 1 THE SIX PHASES OF YOUR CAREER

Citrin, James M. "How Do Careers Really Work? The Three Phases." Influencer Post. *LinkedIn Blog*, October 4, 2012.

———. "A New Lifetime Framework for Your Career." Influencer Post. *LinkedIn Blog*, January 7, 2014.

Citrin, James M., and Richard A. Smith. *The Five Patterns of Extraordinary Careers*. New York: Crown Business, 2003.

CHAPTER 2 THE CAREER TRIANGLE: JOB, COMPENSATION, AND LIFESTYLE

Johnson O'Connor Research Foundation. Home page. http://www.jocrf.org/.
Nemko, Marty. "Why Following Your Passion Can Backfire." *Psychology Today*, March 20, 2014. http://www.psychologytoday.com/blog/how-do-life/201403/why-following-your-passion-can-backfire.

CHAPTER 3 WHAT ABOUT MONEY?

Citrin, James M. "How to Make a Lot of (or at Least Enough) Money." Influencer Post. *LinkedIn Blog*, September 25, 2014.
Stein, Ben. "O.K., Freshmen, It's Time to Study the Real World." *New York Times*, August 28, 2005. http://www.nytimes.com/2005/08/28/business/28every.html?pagewanted=all&module=Search&mabReward=relbias%3As&_r=0.

CHAPTER 4 THE POWER OF RELATIONSHIPS AND NETWORKS

Barker, Eric. "The 10 Best Networking Tips for People Who Hate Networking." The Week. *Barking up the Wrong Tree*, August 8, 2014.
Beatty, Kimberly. "Jobfully Online." *Jobfully Blog*, July

1, 2010, http://blog.jobfully.com/2010/07/the-math
-behind-the-networking-claim/.

Ferrazzi, Keith. *Never Eat Alone: And Other Secrets to Success, One Relationship at a Time.* New York: Crown Business, 2005.

Grant, Adam. "Finding the Hidden Value in Your Network." *LinkedIn Pulse,* June 17, 2013. https://www.linkedin.com/pulse/article/20130617112202-69244073-finding-the-hidden-value-in-your-network.

———. *Give and Take: A Revolutionary Approach to Success.* New York: Viking, 2013.

Uzzi, Brian, and Sharon Dunlap. "How to Build Your Network." *Harvard Business Review,* December 2005.

Wiseman, Richard. *59 Seconds: Think a Little, Change a Lot.* New York: Alfred A. Knopf, 2009.

CHAPTER 6 OVERCOMING THE PERMISSION PARADOX: YOU CAN'T GET THE JOB WITHOUT EXPERIENCE, BUT YOU CAN'T GET EXPERIENCE WITHOUT THE JOB

Citrin, James M. "How to Get the Job When You Don't Have the Experience." Influencer Post. *LinkedIn Blog,* August 11, 2014.

CHAPTER 7 YOU'VE STUDIED LIBERAL ARTS, NOW WHAT?

Bérubé, Michael. "The Humanities, Declining? Not According to the Numbers." *Chronicle of Higher Education,* July 1, 2013. http://chronicle.com/article/The-Humanities-Declining-Not/140093/.

Goudreau, Jenna. "The 15 Most Valuable College Majors."

Forbes.com, May 15, 2012. http://www.forbes.com/sites/jennagoudreau/2012/05/15/best-top-most-valuable-college-majors-degrees/.

Mims, Christopher. "Programming Is a Trade; Let's Train Accordingly." *Wall Street Journal*, August 5, 2014.

Roth, Michael. *Beyond the University: Why Liberal Education Matters*. New Haven, CT: Yale University Press, 2014.

Weinberg, Cory. "Four Years Out, the Great Recession's College Grads Fared Well—If They Picked the Right Major." *Bloomberg Businessweek*, July 10, 2014.

CHAPTER 8 THE ART OF THE INTERVIEW

Citrin, James M. "The Undercover Interviewer: 'Do You Have Any Questions for Me?'" Influencer Post. *LinkedIn Blog*, February 24, 2014.

———. "The Undercover Interviewer: My Single Best Interview Tip." Influencer Post. *LinkedIn Blog*, January 26, 2014.

———. "The Undercover Interviewer: 'Why Should I Hire an Art History Major When I Can Hire a Finance Major?'" Influencer Post. *LinkedIn Blog*, March 3, 2014.

CHAPTER 9 DECIDING WHAT JOB TO ACCEPT

Citrin, James M. "Should You Look for the Right Job or the Right Company?" Influencer Post. *LinkedIn Blog*, June 15, 2014.

"I Have a Best Friend at Work: The Twelve Key Dimensions That Describe Great Workgroups." *Gallup Business Journal*, May 26, 1999. http://www.gallup.com/businessjournal/511/item-10-best-friend-work.aspx.

CHAPTER 10 GETTING OFF TO THE RIGHT START IN A
NEW JOB

Citrin, James M. "A Small but Important Piece of Advice
for Aspiring Young Women Professionals—Be Able to
Talk Sports." Influencer Post. *LinkedIn Blog,* August 7,
2014.

D'Alessandro, David F. *Career Warfare: 10 Rules for Building a Successful Personal Brand and Fighting to Keep It.*
New York: McGraw Hill, 2004.

Neff, Thomas J., and James M. Citrin. *You're in Charge, Now
What?* New York: Crown Business, 2005.

Murray, Charles. *The Curmudgeon's Guide to Getting Ahead.*
New York: Crown Business, 2014.

CHAPTER 11 FOUR GUARANTEED STRATEGIES FOR
SUCCESS

Branson, Sir Richard. *Business Stripped Bare: Adventures of
a Global Entrepreneur.* London: Virgin Books, 2009.

Citrin, James M. "Big Idea 2014: The One Crucial Leadership Skill Is Agility." Influencer Post. *LinkedIn Blog,*
December 10, 2013.

———. "The No. 1 Lesson from Navy SEALs: 'Don't Quit
in Anticipation of Future Failure.'" Influencer Post.
LinkedIn Blog, May 7, 2014.

CHAPTER 12 YOU'RE A KNIGHT, NOT A BISHOP (OR,
HOW TO MOVE FROM JOB TO JOB)

Citrin, James M. "To Jump or Not To Jump, That Is the
Question—How to Think about Whether to Join a Start-
Up." Influencer Post. *LinkedIn Blog,* December 10, 2012.

Gage, Deborah. "The Venture Capital Secret: 3 Out of 4 Start-Ups Fail." *Wall Street Journal*, September 20, 2012.

Xavier, Jon. "75% of Startups Fail, but It's No Biggie." *Silicon Valley Business Journal*, September 21, 2012.

CHAPTER 14 HOW TO CULTIVATE A MENTOR

Allen, Tammy D., Mark L. Poteet, and Susan M. Burroughs. "The Mentor's Perspective: A Qualitative Inquiry and Future Research Agenda." *Journal of Vocational Behavior* 51, no. 1 (1997).

Citrin, James M. "The Undercover Mentor: How to Cultivate an Advisor and Advocate." Influencer Post. *LinkedIn Blog*, March 17, 2014.

Sandberg, Sheryl. *Lean In for Graduates*. New York: Alfred A. Knopf, 2014.

National Humanities Center. "Benjamin Franklin's Junto Club and Lending Library of Philadelphia." National Humanities Center Resource Toolbox, under "Becoming American: The British Atlantic Colonies, 1690–1763," 2008. http://nationalhumanitiescenter.org/pds/becomingamer/ideas/text4/juntolibrary.pdf.

CONCLUSION: ONWARD TO SUCCESS AND HAPPINESS

Branson, Sir Richard. "What's the Best Measurement for Success? Happiness." Influencer Post. *LinkedIn Blog*, November 9, 2012. https://www.linkedin.com/pulse/article/20121109141247-204068115-what-s-the-best-measurement-for-success-happiness?trk=mp-reader-card.

Citrin, James M. "Success and Happiness: Think About the Most Successful Person You Know . . ." Influencer Post. *LinkedIn Blog,* March 31, 2014.

Dolan, Paul. *Happiness by Design: Change What You Do, Not How You Think.* New York: Hudson Street Press, 2014.

Gladwell, Malcolm. *David and Goliath: Underdogs, Misfits, and the Art of Battling Giants.* New York: Little, Brown, 2013.

Leonsis, Ted. *The Business of Happiness.* Washington, DC: Regnery, 2010.

Acknowledgments

In August 2013, I received a call from the leadership of Indiana University Alumni Association (IUAA). At the time, I didn't have any connection to IU and I certainly wasn't a Hoosier. However, Caroline Dowd-Higgins, IUAA's director of alumni professional enrichment, and a leading author, career coach, and media personality on all aspects of careers, and Deborah Collins Stephens, cofounder for the Center for Innovative Leadership, also an author and executive in residence at IUAA, had an exciting idea. They were doing extensive research on career strategies as part of IU's efforts to serve the nearly six hundred thousand IU graduates in over 150 countries. They were big fans of the book I had coauthored in 2003, *The Five Patterns of Extraordinary Careers*, and suggested that I write a similar book on career strategies dedicated to current college students and recent graduates. Their enthusiasm for the topic was immediately infectious and tapped into my own passion for the topic that is based on trying to be a source of sound career advice for my own three kids, all in their twenties. Hence, *The Career Playbook* was born. Thanks to Caroline and Deborah, and also J. T. Forbes, executive director and CEO of the IUAA. I've benefited from their encouragement and support all along the way.

This project never could have been accomplished without the partnership of my Spencer Stuart colleague, the talented and indefatigable Kate Ashforth. A star senior associate in our Technology, Media, and Telecommunications Practice, Kate, a 2008 graduate of Brown University, is as passionate about career strategies, mentorship, and professional success as I am. She helped construct and analyze the detailed surveys that were at the foundation of the research for this book. She participated in hundreds of interviews and served as a true thought partner from concept to execution, offering detailed commentary in every chapter. I cannot thank you enough, Kate.

I also benefited enormously from the brilliant and dedicated efforts of Spencer Stuart summer intern Adrian Kerester. Adrian, a member of the Middlebury College class of 2015, showed how a young professional can add value over and above all reasonable hopes and expectations. She took hold of the survey research and sliced and diced the numbers in every imaginable way to tease out the most important insights. She wrote thought pieces on the career issues that give college students the greatest anxieties today. And she led the process of engaging with the directors of career services at the colleges and universities with whom we worked. Thank you, Adrian!

With this book, unlike my previous books, I had the benefit of Dan Roth and his talented editorial and content team at LinkedIn. I am proud to be a LinkedIn Influencer; having the ability to test out and explore ideas with the vibrant and constructive LinkedIn community of readers has been incredibly helpful in framing and sharpening my ideas. Thanks as well to all the members of the LinkedIn community who have read my various posts and offered the thousands of thoughtful comments and insights.

I would like to acknowledge and thank Spencer Stuart,

my treasured firm, which for the past twenty-one years has
provided me with the support, encouragement, and professional freedom to do my work and also pursue a passion
project such as *The Career Playbook*. This book has had
more involvement from colleagues across our firm than all
my other books combined. I was able to present the book
and get detailed feedback from fifty of our analysts and associates. Beyond this group, Ben Machtiger, our chief marketing and strategy officer, read the manuscript and offered
invaluable and detailed comments to help strike the right
balance of encouragement and reality. Rich Kurkowski,
our chief financial officer, and Dave Rasmussen, our general counsel, have as always provided the important support
for establishing the publishing contracts and performing a
legal review. Kevin Connelly, our managing partner and
CEO, also read the manuscript as it was approaching final
form and offered important advice and strong encouragement. In addition, a wide array of my partners contributed
their expertise to provide advice to aspiring young professionals, specifically Cathy Anterasian, Jason Baumgarten,
Lauren Callaghan, David Daniel, Julie Daum, Chris Free-
man, Amanda Granson, Susan Hart, Claudia Kelly, Alex
Kloppenberg, Lindsay Meyers, Tom Neff, Dayton Ogden,
Greg Sedlock, Melissa Stone, and Rebecca Thornton.

And my Spencer Stuart life would not be possible without the partnership and friendship of my executive assistant, Karen Steinegger. Of all the books she has helped me
with over the years, this is the one that has sparked her enthusiasm most, and for that I am deeply appreciative.

There are few topics among business leaders, not-for-
profit executives, and college and university presidents and

officers as close to the heart as career advice for young people. Because of people's absolute commitment to trying to help improve the careers and lives of young people around the world, I was able to draw on the wisdom and experience of a wide range of leaders. I am especially grateful to the following, who have participated in this project with a spirit of generosity: Beth Axelrod, eBay; Stacy Bingham, Vassar College; Laszlo Bock, Google; Joe Bosch, DIRECTV; Sir Richard Branson, Virgin Group; Steve Burke, NBC Universal; Sharon Belden Castonguay, Wesleyan University; Laura Chambers, eBay; Beth Comstock, General Electric; Chad Dickerson, Etsy; Angelina Dolan; John Donahoe, eBay; Patrick Doyle, Domino's; Deborah Dugan, Product (RED); Keith Ferrazzi, Ferrazzi Greenlight; Tom Freston, formerly of Viacom and adventurer extraordinaire; Stephen Friedman, MTV; Tony Galbato, Amazon.com; Malcolm Gladwell, *The New Yorker*; Lori Goler, Facebook; Stacie Hagenbaugh, Smith College; Kristen Hamilton, Koru; Bonnie Hammer, NBC Universal; Frans Hijkoop, MetLife; Cappy Hill, Vassar College; Andy Jennings, Vassar College; Little Johnny, Pebble Beach Resorts; Hubert Joly, Best Buy; Don Kjelleren, Middlebury College; Ted Leonsis, Washington Capitals; Dan Loeb, Third Point Advisors; Michael Lynton, Sony; Gail McGovern, American Red Cross; Susan Monaghan, Sonos; Jill O'Donnell-Tormey, Cancer Research Institute; Eric Olson, U.S. Navy; Jennifer Opalacz, Wesleyan University; Sandi Peterson, Johnson & Johnson; Carol Robinette, American Red Cross; Michael Roth, Wesleyan University; Sheryl Sandberg, Facebook; Mike Sciola, Colgate University; Guhan Selvaretnam, Discovery Communications; Clara Shih, Hearsay Social; Sanyin Siang, Duke

University; Jay Walker, Walker Digital; Wendell Weeks, Corning; Mike White, DIRECTV; Barbara-Jan Wilson, Wesleyan University; Roger Woolsey, Dartmouth College; Woody Young, Lazard; and Strauss Zelnick, Zelnick Media.

Perhaps the most valuable—and certainly the most enjoyable—part of this book came from working so closely with a large group of young professionals. They have helped shape the agenda by sharing what's most on their minds about careers. They completed surveys, provided anecdotes, reacted to chapters and ideas, provided detailed commentary, and generally helped keep me on track. I hope the experience wasn't too painful for them and that it perhaps added some value to their own careers. I benefited invaluably from the work and devotion of my niece and nephews, Alex Citrin, Andrew Citrin, Charlie Citrin, and Ryan Lane, as well as from the input, advice, and stories of dear friends and clever collaborators Haley Sacks, Tori McKenna, and Taylor Clark. I also drew heavily on the input and advice of Nicki Softness, Jamie Greenberg, Natalia Gonzalez, Caroline Hart, Clare Ashforth, Amanda Facelle, Eric Spector, Andrew Spalter, Andrew Marcelle, Fergus Campbell, and Catherine Donahoe.

I would also like to thank my incredibly devoted team at Crown, who have believed in this book since our first conversation. Roger Scholl and Derek Reed have been demanding and thoughtful editors but always hugely value-adding partners in this process. Thanks also to Tina Constable, whose inspiring leadership at Crown has ensured that the book could get the priority and resources to bring it to readers in time to hopefully help young professionals as they go about launching their careers. My thanks also go to the state-of-the-art publishing, publicity, and marketing teams at Crown: Campbell Wharton, Megan Perritt, Ayelet Gruenspecht, and Owen Haney.

This is my seventh book, and from the very start in 1997 Rafe Sagalyn has been my literary agent. He has been steadfast in his support for my work and has become not only a wise and trusted counselor and partner but a cherished friend as well.

I would like to offer a special thank-you to Annalora von Pentz, an enormously talented twenty-two-year-old illustrator and graphics designer. Annalora dove into the book with enthusiasm, responsiveness, and a strong artistic and conceptual perspective. She was responsible for each and every chart, sketch, and graphic in the book.

My deepest appreciation goes to my family for their enthusiastic support of this book from inception to reality. My parents, Glenna and Hal Citrin, my brother and sister-in-law Jeff and Rona Citrin, and my sister and brother-in-law Nancy and Ken Lane not only have read, discussed, and debated the contents and ideas in this book but have been with me during weekends and vacations while I was being antisocial and working on the manuscript. They also took delight when their kids and grandkids engaged in the topic, including not only Alex, Andrew, and Charlie Citrin but also Ryan, Harry, and Sylvie Lane. They and a small number of special friends along the way have provided the continuity and love and guidance that have been truly essential during the past couple of years.

Finally, and most important, I'd like to thank my children, Teddy, Oliver, and Lily, to whom this book is dedicated. Teddy and Oliver, both college graduates over the past three years, have been deeply involved in the conception, shaping, editing, and storytelling throughout this book. Along with Lily, still a college student, who participated in a roundtable discussion about the book with twenty fellow undergraduates, they have let me test out my advice on them and their friends. They have provided hard-hitting and always constructive feedback. I love them with all my heart and have cherished the opportunity that this book has afforded to share an important project.

Index

ABOUT THE AUTHOR

Jim Citrin leads Spencer Stuart's CEO Practice and serves on the firm's worldwide board of directors. A noted expert on leadership and CEO succession, Jim has published seven books, including the worldwide bestsellers *You're in Charge, Now What?* and *The Five Patterns of Extraordinary Careers.*

Throughout his twenty-one years at Spencer Stuart, Jim has completed more than 575 CEO, board director, and top management searches for leading media, technology, and communications consumer and private equity–backed companies, as well as for major not-for-profit institutions. Examples include the CEOs of ADP, AMC Entertainment, Best Buy, Boston Properties, CNN Worldwide, Discovery Communications, Dun & Bradstreet, eBay, Electronic Arts, FICO, Gartner, the Green Bay Packers, Harris, Hulu, Intel, MetLife, MIT Media Lab, the New York Public Library, the New York Times Company, Nielsen, One Kings Lane, PayPal, Pitney Bowes, Product (RED), the RAND Corporation, Reader's Digest Association, Sesame Workshop, Shazam, Sirius XM, Starwood Hotels & Resorts, Starz, Univision, Walmart.com, Willis Group, and Yahoo!, and board directors running the gamut from Amazon.com, eBay, Microsoft, and Facebook to the American Red Cross, Etsy, and the International Tennis Hall of Fame.

Jim graduated Phi Beta Kappa from Vassar College and served as a trustee on their board for twelve years. Currently, he is a trustee at Wesleyan University and on the boards of the International Tennis Hall of Fame and the Cancer Research Institute. He obtained his MBA from Harvard Business School, graduating with distinction. Jim started his career as an analyst at Morgan Stanley and after business school was an associate at Goldman Sachs and then McKinsey before starting at Spencer Stuart in 1994.

Jim lives in Connecticut and has three children, Teddy, Oliver, and Lily.

Career Advice
from the Executive Placement Guru
James M. Citrin

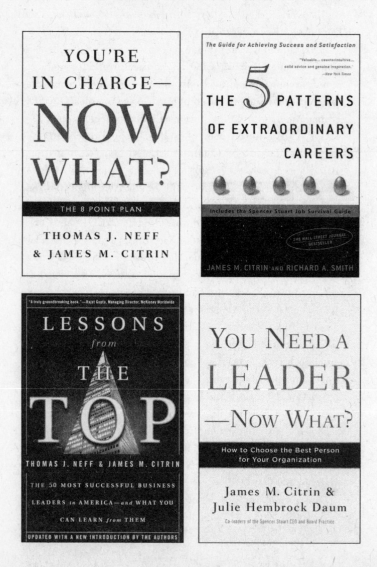